The ANGEL CHRONICLES:

True Stories of Angelic Experiences

The Annunciation: The Angel Gabriel.
Gaudenzio Ferrari. C. 1470-1546. Public Domain.

STARR RAE KNIGHTE

Dedication

To those who believe, and to those who are about to.

Angels. Raffaello Sanzio. (Detail of The Sistine Madonna).1512-1514. Public Domain.

TABLE OF CONTENTS

Introduction	1
Feathers and Block Party Angels	13
The Beginning Days	15
An Engagement Ring and Monarch Butterflies	17
My Near-Death Experience and Devotion to Saint Michael	19
Looking Back with Some Help from Saint Michael	25
My Mother's Remarkable Hospital Experience	29
Our Saint Michael Statue	32
The Salad Bar Angels	33
Angel from India	35
Shopping with the Angels	37
My Mother's Move	39
Downtown Angel Signs	41
Electronics and Angels	43
A Brown, Furry-Tailed Angel	44
God Answers in Mysterious Ways	46
Hurricane Sandy Angels	49
A Message to Comfort	52
An Angel Feather for a Neighbor	54
Angels at the Rainbow Bridge	56
Bicycle Angels	60
The Angel Bracelet	62
Angel in the Church Pew	64

Cemetery Angels 66

Orchids and Angels 68

Heavenly Patio Furniture 70

A Warning Sent 71

God's Time Is Always Right 73

Larry the Homeless Angel 75

Do Angels Have Backups? 78

My Saint Michael Poster for the Women's Retreat 80

ADORO Angels 82

Rooftop Angels 84

Messages on Facebook 85

A Message from Heaven 87

Footsteps on a beach 90

Saint Michael's Approval 92

Message on a Sidewalk 94

An Angelic Eternity Scarf 95

Heart-Shaped Boxes and Angel Feathers 97

My Husband's Work Van 99

An Angel Kiss During the Night 100

Angels at the Wheel 101

Lost and Found 104

Cat-Man Bob 106

If You Listen, You Can Hear the Angels Sing 109

The Snow Angels of Manitoba 112

A Man and a Pillow 114

Angels Watching over Us 116

Saint Michael on the Internet 118

Feathers, Woodpeckers, and Good Friends 120

My Mother's Battle with Cancer and Beatific Death 122

Bagpipes and Grasshoppers 127

Message from a Cardinal 128

The Copper Bracelet 129

Message in the Sky 130

Angel in the Waiting Room 132

Lest You Dash Yourself 134

The Mysterious Angel Card 135

Various Occurrences 136

A Visit to Saint Michael's Basilica 138

In Loving Memory of Pam 140

Feathers and Block Party Angels Revisited 142

In Loving Memory of Janet and Richie 143

The Saint Michael Prayer 148

The Chaplet of Saint Michael (Rosary of the Angels) 149

Angel of God Prayer 152

About the Author 155

Editor's Note

The Angel Chronicles
MAY 2021

This is a book about the author's multiple encounters with angels of God. It is a moving, awe-inspiring group of stories. The author shows an awareness of the world around her that is amazing, and she willingly and openly helps readers to learn to recognize the interactions they may be having themselves on a daily basis.

This book has a powerful message about the love of God, the power and helpfulness of angels, and the importance of sharing with and loving our fellow human beings and animals. This is an important message for our time.

Acknowledgments

Dr. Zal and Josie, your encouragement is the reason why my stories are no longer sitting on a shelf. You believed they could be brought to life one day and taught me to believe in myself.

Deacon Bill, your guidance helped place me in the driver's seat for this long, incredible journey.

Steven, for encouraging me to "Never lose sight!"

Peggy, for putting up with the electronic madness and for your patience, advice, and guidance.

My beloved cousin Angel, for shielding what was left of my sanity. I can't thank you enough for your patience and for the many hours you guided me through this labyrinth. I have been twice blessed and am grateful that God directed us back together after all these years.

"Earth Angels" in my stories. Without you, these pages would be empty. Because of you, my mission was not only educational but healing as well: Angelina, Ashithra, Rita, Dan and Pam, Charlene, Moms and Dads, Donna, Ally and Evan, Rose, Sophia, Clement, Chris, June and Pedro, Mr. and Mrs. J, Ric, Larry, "Cat-man" Bob, Jim, Kelly, Kim and Pat, Daria and Melissa, Donna, Fely, April, Colleen, Diane, Linda and Wes, Cathy, Carmela, Marie, Heather, Richie, and Janet.

My intercessory prayer group: Linda, Tina, Luisa, Denise, Linda, Mary, Betty, Gerry, Diane, Ann, Anne, and Wink for your acceptance, love, guidance, support, and wisdom.

Monsignor Tom, for your permission to use the Church and statue photos, and especially for all of your hard work and dedication to our wonderful parish.

Tommy, my number one "Earth Angel," for your love and great sense of humor, which keeps me grounded. Thanks for helping me carry my cross when I could not carry it alone.

Photo: Angel statue/planter.

With much sadness, we were informed that Dr. Zal had passed away during the last stages of publishing this book. Another one of God's "Earth Angels" was called home.

May he forever rest in peace.

Introduction

H AVE YOU EVER felt a presence, or experienced a situation that could not be logically explained? How about mysterious happenings surrounding you or your loved ones? Have you heard that angels can bring us messages in dreams, visions, and signs?

Do you ever wonder if there is a way to recognize them in your own daily life situations, and if there is a way to safely discern between the good and evil spirits who are competing to get your attention?

Many years ago, I had a near-death experience, and my life was miraculously saved with no logical explanation of what happened to me. I am still here for reasons I believe are beyond human understanding. Someday, God will provide us with a thorough explanation of why it happened.

This collection of stories is made up of my experiences, experiences that, to most,

Photo: Bronze angel statue. Used with permission.

would seem like casual, everyday events. But for myself, whether through some type of heavenly intervention or an openness of mind and heart, these life circumstances have given me such things as faith, hope, comfort, inspiration, warning, discernment, and peace. When visual signs materialize during a specific time, within the boundaries of a particular event, the ordinary can no longer be seen as coincidental. Our senses tell us that something profound is underway.

By sharing these various occurrences, I hope to stimulate an awareness of the spiritual realm that either guides or misguides us. From what I have witnessed, I believe, acknowledge, and am grateful for having an awareness of the presence of Almighty God and for the miraculous intervention and protection of His Holy Angels and their Chief Commander, Saint Michael the Archangel.

Originally, this book came about because I felt inclined to share these personal and spiritual encounters with angels with my friends and family. However, I seriously believe God had another plan. He sent me on a mission to expand and share these experiences with many others, to bring them closer to Him as they did for me. They helped me to cope with our many earthly challenges, through observations and miraculous appearances of dispensed heavenly grace. The messages we receive in daily life or dreams that some would call coincidental or unexplained happenings are at times simply events that are just beyond our human comprehension. Nonetheless, if these messages are received with faith in God's will, they can relieve us of stress and build up our strength in knowing that help is not far beyond but is indeed within reach. Reading these stories may enable you to relate to your own personal experiences and bring some realization of the graces that are sent from God, especially during times of tribulation. God's Holy Angels want to be acknowledged and called upon for assistance, in God's name. We oftentimes forget or neglect to be grateful for the many blessings we receive from our Almighty Creator. May these stories remind you that you are children of God and that His benevolence and love is everlasting. May they lift your spirit and send joy into your heart.

I am not an expert on angelology. My goal is to witness and share what I have received through these events, sometimes using quotes from scripture that I felt directly applied to what I experienced at the time. These are stories from my personal life, which were kept in a diary for twenty-five years, of my experiences of good and evil spirits surrounding us.

These displays have left no doubt in my mind that these spirits cross our paths daily. It is important to know that if we call upon either, they will hear and eagerly respond. Countless times, the good angels have intervened in my life to direct, warn, or comfort me, especially when the evil ones were doing their best to influence me to turn from integrity.

Hatred for man's unity is the root cause for the evil spirits to do anything in their power to separate us and make us hate one another. Their goal is to make mankind sink into total despair and bring an end to brotherly love and goodness. Only God's Holy Warrior Angels will guide, protect, and inspire us to perform the work God has so lovingly created us to do.

It is crucial, particularly in these unsettling times, to cultivate an awareness of the evil spirits among us. They will do anything they can to steer us away from God's love and to influence us to not live a life of virtue.

Unfortunately, many of us are still innocently blind to the dangers out there. Satan can disguise himself as an angel of light, and his evil cohorts can easily manipulate the truth to deceive us while appearing to be good, friendly, and helpful. There are many ways they can lead us into a trap of demonic activity and even full demonic possession, if we allow it. This can happen mostly when we try to foretell the future or try to contact the dead. They know that, as humans, we have weaknesses they can take advantage of, knowing we can effortlessly be fooled into believing we have contacted the dead when they can disguise themselves as our deceased loved ones. The evil spirits, just like the Holy Angels, possess the ability to be present, but to be unperceived, felt, or heard.

We need to be aware of how easy it can be to open a portal by calling out to spirits other than God. Once they gain access, these unwelcomed guests are hard to get rid of, because we have unknowingly invited them in. Both sides await, eager to answer our call.

Other ways evil spirits can snare us are fortunetelling, tarot/angel cards, palm readings, crystal balls, séances, Ouija boards, or anything spiritual. We must remember that God is in control, and only he knows what lies in the future.

When I was growing up, some kids thought a Ouija board was one of the coolest things to own. They thought doing séances and levitations, going to fortune-tellers, and reading tarot cards were fun. Few families knew much about the spiritual world back then or comprehended the danger it invited into their homes. If parents were warned about it, they may have laughed or shrugged it off as just silly superstition. Totally unaware, they thought their kids were just getting together to have some innocent fun. Unfortunately, their lack of knowledge could come with a price.

Scripture states, "Let there not be found among you anyone who causes their son or daughter to pass through the fire, or practices divination, or is a soothsayer, augur, or sorcerer or who casts spells, consults ghosts and spirits, or seeks oracles from the dead. Anyone who does such things is an abomination to the Lord, and because of such abominations the Lord, your God, is dispossessing them before you." (Deuteronomy 18:10) (NABRE).

A woman who was involved in a few of these occult practices during her early teen years revealed something frightening that went on inside her parent's house: strange occurrences began as time went on. Preferring to remain anonymous, I will refer to her as Angelina.

Angelina joked about the dark cloud hovering over her parent's

house. There were constant obstacles and burdensome situations. Things would malfunction or break for bizarre, unknown reasons. The ambience in her home was always erratic, causing much anger, frustration, and conflict in her family. Her father was a war veteran who suffered from Post-Traumatic Stress Disorder. His introversion held him back from venturing out much, preferring the safety of the couch,

Photo: Temptation on the Mount. Duccio di Buoninsegna. 1308-11. Public Domain.

glued to the television, trying to drown out the demons that haunted him. Angelina wondered if he was aware of the alcoholism that had crept up on him.

Her mother was in complete denial and refused to talk about it, as she suffered physically, emotionally, and mentally herself. Most of her burden was hidden from all who knew her, even from her closest family members. She did not spend much time around the family either, often confining herself to her bedroom to watch her own television programs. Family life was dysfunctional, detached, and distant. No one spoke much. Angelina felt like she was walking on eggshells from the uneasiness she was forced to live with in her family.

Later in life, Angelina developed a better understanding of why these strange things happened in her parent's home. As a teenager, however, she was fighting her own demons as she tried to shut out her own emptiness and smother the depression she was developing inside. As an older adult, she discovered that her mother's burden was what a psychiatrist confirmed to be a personality disorder, a mental disorder exhibited by unhealthy ongoing dysfunctional behaviors, moods, and self-image. This explained why growing up and becoming an adult in her mother's presence became such a challenge. The effort to be a good daughter was a struggle, so Angelina sought escapes, hoping to smother the pain and loss of not having an available, nurturing mother in her life. Residing in a tough neighborhood, she often had to deal with bullies at school, which did not help matters. A negative attitude toward her parent's church developed. She referred to all the parishioners as the holier-than-thou crowd, viewing them as a bunch of hypocrites who thought they were better than everyone else. The unrealistic conviction made her feel ostracized and unloved, leading to more anger and depression. Evil spirits began to control her life as she turned away from God, no longer worshiping or thanking Him for His blessings. It felt like He had nothing to offer her, and she thought it seemed absurd to go to church. Her parents did not seem to be there for her, and neither was He.

Angelina was unaware that she would need God's help more than ever, but she blindly walked away from it, which opened a bigger portal, and Satan had some dirty work to do. Her life became filled with depression and anxiety, although she claimed to be pretty damned good at hiding it. After years of suppression, she developed ongoing health issues and financial problems. All of the unhealthy relationships she settled for caused her life to go into a downward spiral.

One day, she realized she could not do it alone and decided to invite God back into her life. She went back to His Church to ask for help. He sent sisters and brothers to help her fight the battle against Satan and his demons, which had invaded her life. She could not believe how these people loved and accepted her for who she was, a lost and broken soul.

Photo: Tommy during a sunset.

Accepting God's mercy, forgiveness, and grace led her back into His light. These people He put in her path knew the faith, lived it, and truly practiced it. They were a huge surprise to her, nothing like the hypocrites she imagined in the past. They were true disciples of Christ, who "talked the talk and walked the walk." Angelina discovered a lasting peace, which could only come from God.

"Thou hast made us for thyself, O Lord, and our heart is restless until it finds its rest in thee." —Augustine of Hippo.

Looking back, she saw God in His great mercy putting the right people in her life. The moral code of these spiritual warriors who stayed by her side, no matter what she foolishly said or did, guided her in fighting the war to get her life, and her faith, back.

Gradually, Angelina's life changed for the better and many blessings came. She met a wonderful man and they got married, plus her health and financial situation started to improve. She found happiness from deep within her heart and soul.

Perhaps, this is what they refer to as being saved.

I often joked of writing a book about my incredible angelic experiences for family and friends. Looking back on past years, a divine influence must have prompted me to write down these stories in a diary that eventually were compiled into this book to share with others. I joked about it, but from my mouth to God's ears, as he took my joking seriously! The years passed and He must have gotten tired of waiting for it to materialize. I can imagine Him dropping His foot down, sending a Divine swift kick to my gluteus maximus!

His Holy Angels had to be fed up with me also. All of those wonderful stories of them, collecting dust on a shelf, with no one to read the stories, that would possibly bring some hope into this mixed-up world! I bet they probably wanted to do some serious gluteus maximus kicking themselves. However, because they were created by God to be merciful, they probably just pleaded with God for assistance to somehow deal with the quirky redhead below. God had a better idea than kicking my butt. He sent some Earth Angels instead. So, it happened.

One year at an annual Fourth of July Block Party, I joked again to a neighbor about writing a book about angels after finding out that he wrote and published a few books himself. He expressed interest in reading my stories, so I loaned them to him to read. Afterward, he encouraged me to make them available for the public. If it weren't for this pivotal meeting between neighbors, my stories would still be sitting on a shelf in our house, rounding up dust bunnies.

God then strategically placed more special people on my path. These Earth Angels supported and guided me through many chaotic, overwhelming hours, trying to figure out how I would put all of these stories together. At the time, I had very limited computer skills and was aware of how vulnerable my lack of skills would render me, knowing full well that Satan, lurking in the shadows with his ulterior motives, did not want this information out there. He would call upon his demons to do whatever it would take to make sure my efforts would end up as nothing but a complete failure.

I wonder if he had any idea that his cohorts would be dealing with an extremely stubborn woman who would not give up on her mission. A woman who, at times, would admittedly cuss a bit, stomp her feet, and cry her eyes out, then ask God for forgiveness, strength, and the wisdom to complete this task. Could he have guessed that despite all the stress and aggravation he would send her way, that in the long run she would still refuse to lose hope and quit?

"For this I work and struggle, in accord with the exercise of his power working within me." (Colossians 1:29) (NABRE).

I left it in God's hands. If He wanted it done, He would provide a way, and send the information that I needed. He would send protection and help. He would send His Holy Warrior Angels.

"The angel of the Lord encamps around those who fear him, and he saves them. Taste and see that the Lord is good; blessed is the stalwart one who takes refuge in him. Fear the Lord, you his holy ones; nothing is lacking to those who fear him. The rich grow poor and go hungry, but those who seek the Lord lack no good thing." (Psalm 34:8–11) (NABRE).

Photo: Photo: Hosts of Angels by Guariento Di Arpo. 1338-1377. Public Domain.

The Bible informs us that angels have been with us since the beginning of time, when God created the world. Their front-row seats in Heaven allowed them to witness this spectacular event. They observed creation forming out of complete darkness, the sun bringing light to the first day, and the glow of the moon on the first night. Then oceans, continents, rivers, lakes, ponds, and streams forming, along with majestic mountains.

"Where were you when I founded the earth? Tell me, if you have understanding. Who determined its size? Surely you know? Who stretched out the measuring line for it? Into what were its pedestals sunk, and who laid its cornerstone, while the morning stars sang together and all the sons of God shouted for joy?" (Job 38:4-7) (NABRE).

Everything was going just fine, until one of God's Angels allowed his pride and arrogance to blind him of God's supremacy. He wanted to be in charge, to own the beauty God created, and he could care less about God's plans. His name was Lucifer. He turned against God, became evil, and battled against Saint Michael the Archangel—the leader of God's good Angels—who stayed loyal to God. The angels were given free will, so they were allowed to choose between good and evil. Some decided to follow Lucifer (also called Satan) and become evil. This is why humans and God's creatures are born in a world of benevolent and malevolent spirits.

"Then war broke out in heaven; Michael and his angels battled against the dragon. The dragon and its angels fought back, but they did not prevail and there was no longer any place for them in heaven." (Revelation 12:7-8) (NABRE).

Imagine the violence at that pivotal point in time. All of the magnificence and serenity of the heavens and earth disrupted by a war between good and evil angels. It caused the loveliness of God's creation to be tainted by the wickedness of the creatures he loved enough to bring into existence.

Lucifer and the rebellious angels were defeated by Saint Michael and God's Holy Angels, then thrown from Heaven down to earth. Since then, their ambition to rule the world has never ended, so the fight between the good and evil spirits (angels) continues to this day.

"The huge dragon, the ancient serpent, who is called the Devil and Satan, who deceived the whole world, was thrown down to earth, and its angels were thrown down with it." (Revelation 12:9) (NABRE).

This battle of utter chaos between the good and evil angels must have easily blown away any late-night action movie. Although it occurred at the beginning of time, it is in the last book of the Bible, called Revelation, an account of the symbolic visions of an apocalypse, written by John, who is believed to be one of Jesus's apostles.

Lucifer and his demons are persistent. They incite war, havoc, and hatred, promote evil in humans, and are hell bent (excuse the pun!) on doing anything in their power to offend God by turning us against Him. By sending suffering with the intent to turn us away from God's Grace, they deceive us into believing God does not even exist. By spreading lies and hatred, their attacks on their victims' minds are cunning and completely invisible. From conception until death, one's entire life is spent battling evil.

Why did God give his creatures free will and not just create a perfect world without evil? Maybe He loved his creatures so much that He let them decide if they would love Him or not, without forcing them to love him?

Would you prefer if someone loved you freely of their own free will?

"God in the beginning created human beings and made them subject to their own free choice. If you choose, you can keep the commandments; loyalty is doing the will of God. Set before you are fire and water; to whatever you choose, stretch out your hand. Before everyone are life and death, whichever they choose will be given them." (Sirach 15:14–17) (NAB).

Satan knows about this choice. He knows humanity's weak points, which are his ultimate targets. The sins of pride, covetousness, lust, anger, gluttony, envy, and sloth are encouraged by sending temptations to influence us in the forms of money, prestige, illness, hardships, relationships, addictions, and so on.

Do you think all of the discord sent to us is from God? It is from Satan and the army he recruited from God's Fallen Angels. God is about love, peace, and serenity, not about war, chaos, hatred, and killing. God creates life, but we, as sinful humans, destroy it out of selfishness and gain.

"Before I formed you in the womb I knew you, before you were born I dedicated you, a prophet to the nations I appointed you." (Jeremiah 1:5) (NABRE).

Satan's diabolical plan is to send his army of demons into our minds through these nooks and crannies we are not aware of, turning us into hateful people by sowing division among us, motivating us to hate our brothers and sisters that God created for us to love as ourselves. Yet, there is always hope that the majority of mankind will rise above all of the evil ambitions known only to Satan and his demons, thus allowing Saint Michael and God's Holy Angels to defeat them and win the final war victorious.

As you read my stories, may your spirit be enlightened and inspired, filled with a child-like faith and wonder, knowing that the Holy Angels are here to guide us to observe how love, mercy, and compassion toward all humans and God's creatures is the answer. May you feel the power of God's love and miracles through these pages, and His Holy omnipotent protection through Saint Michael and His army of Holy Warrior Angels.

"Bless the Lord, all you His Angels, mighty in strength, acting at his behest, obedient to his command." (Psalm 103:20) (NABRE)

Photo: Saint Michael expelling Lucifer and the Rebel Angels.
Guariento Di Arpo. 1622. Public Domain.

Feathers and Block Party Angels

W HEN SEARCHING HIGH and low for something that is nowhere to be found, God can motivate an Earth Angel to bring it to you. They suddenly appear at the door one day with whatever it is in their hand, not even knowing you were participating in a wild-goose chase trying to find it. This is an example of the type of event most people would overlook or simply label a coincidence. However, if you think about it, these things happen often. By staying connected with eyes wide open, our Holy Celestial Friends will reveal that they are readily available and eager to help us when they are needed. The way we know this is by their actions. If it is good, and reflects God's mercy, it is from Him and His messengers. You can count on anything steering us to goodness and holiness to be from God and His Holy Angels.

My Saint Michael medallion, unbeknownst to me, fell off my keychain in the supermarket. Prompted to look, I found it on top of one of my grocery bags at the checkout. Then, after loading the groceries into the car and hopping into the driver's seat, somehow my necklace's clasp had come open, and the cross was dangling down upon my chest. Luckily, it did not fall off. It was being held only by the open clasp. I was grateful this happened in the safety of our car and was discovered. It would have caused much distress if the cross and necklace were lost, because they had belonged to my mother. The Saint Michael medallion could be replaced, unlike my mother's cross and necklace. This prompted immediate acknowledgment, thanks, and praise, first to God, then for the mercy and goodness he sends our way via His Holy Angels or our Earth Angel friends.

Two white feathers gracefully floated down out of the sky next to me later that day, while I was doing yard work. *God, what are your plans for me? What do you want me to do with my life? Will you ever reveal it? Will I ever get an answer?*

It seemed like God was always too busy to reply, that my prayers and messages kept going straight to His voicemail. The next day, though, something amazing happened at our annual neighborhood block party. While chatting with a neighbor, who is the author of several books, I jokingly mentioned to him that I had kicked around the idea of writing a book about the angelic experiences I had chronicled in a diary for the past twenty-five years. Genuinely interested, he asked if he could read them. A week after I allowed him to read them, he encouraged me to edit and publish them. At the time, there were fifty stories, but as I started to work on them, more kept coming! Perhaps God sent an Earth Angel into my life to get these stories kick started. I can envision Him, majestically seated upon His throne in Heaven with His long white robe trailing for miles, shouting down to earth something like this to little ole me,

"Enough lollygagging! It is time to get this started!!"

It occurred to me the Holy Angels had been sending messages the whole week: the medallion, the chain and cross, and then the feathers. Were they trying to get my attention, to prepare me for a special mission? We prayed that the Holy Spirit would guide and protect me, deflect Satan's attacks, and send wisdom and strength for what may come, knowing the evil ones would not want this book to be completed. They would not let it be finished without sending any hardships or obstacles. I felt emotions of excitement, nervousness, and fright all at once. Little did I know that this book was destined to become a labor of love.

The Beginning Days

M ANY YEARS AGO, Tommy and I had a beautiful black Labrador retriever named Buddy. We found out he had cancer after he jumped from our parked van and landed on his front leg, breaking it. X-rays revealed the cancer had spread to his bones, which made them brittle, causing the break. The cancer had also spread to his sternum. The choices given by the vet were to amputate his front leg, which might allow him three months to live, or to put him to sleep.

This was a horrific nightmare, because Buddy seemed to be in such great health until this happened. He had great amounts of energy and did not look sick at all. It felt like we had been sucker punched. After a few days, we made the dreadful and heartbreaking decision to put him to sleep. We did not want him to suffer any longer by putting him through surgery, then forcing him to adapt to living with only one front leg. There was no guarantee he would live three more months, let alone survive the surgery.

We will never forget that day, as I gently held his head in my lap, sobbing out loud in my grief. He looked at me with his big brown eyes as if to say, "Mommy, do not be sad, it will be okay. I love you." It was the most difficult decision we have ever had to make, and it haunted me for a long time. It felt like we were playing God, choosing when it was Buddy's time.

Upon our arrival home afterward, we tried to comfort each other, but our tears would not stop. Both of our hearts were broken. Buddy was such a great dog and a beloved member of our family. I prayed to be comforted somehow, knowing that we had made the right decision, that Buddy was no longer suffering and was at peace in Heaven.

Suddenly the phone rang, along with a crash that came from the kitchen. I ran inside to discover an angel suncatcher had fallen from the window into the sink. I reached for it while answering the phone and was surprised to hear the voice of a favorite client calling to offer condolences over the loss of Buddy. She had called my workplace and was given the sad news. Back in the living room, Tommy was awaiting my return and asked who called. I hesitated before responding. It dawned on me that, prior to the phone call, I had prayed for some kind of comfort about Buddy. The phone rang exactly when the angel suncatcher fell. A sympathetic client called to send consolation, and not a moment too soon!

Our hearts sensed that a heavenly message had been sent. Years later, when we lost our beloved Dr. Seuss, the last of our three bearded dragons, we again prayed for comfort in knowing he was at peace and happy in Heaven with his best friend, Buddy. Later in the evening, Tommy was looking at videos of Dr. Seuss and mentioned how much he missed him and the emptiness he felt from seeing the comical, endearing videos. We recalled the angel suncatcher that fell from the window earlier and realized that it was the same one that fell the day Buddy was put to sleep. Did God allow a message to be sent for us to be comforted?

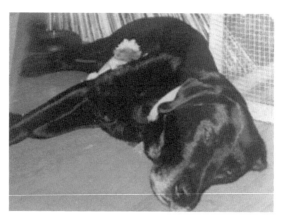

Photo: Two inseparable best friends, Buddy and our bearded dragon Dr. Seuss.
When Buddy broke his leg, Dr. Seuss stayed by his side and refused to leave him.

An Engagement Ring and Monarch Butterflies

M Y HUSBAND SURPRISED me with a marriage proposal and a beautiful engagement ring one lovely summer day as we were hiking on a trail near Dingmans Falls in Pennsylvania. We dodged the high, grassy areas where those evil little buggers called ticks are known to hide, waiting for their meals to be delivered. Eventually we made our way to the top of the mountain and sat down on a big rock to catch our breath. After relaxing and chatting for a while, I asked if he had anything else to say, sensing something was afoot. He got down on his knee, presented the ring, then asked me to marry him.

"Can I think about it?" I asked, but I could not keep a straight face. I kissed him and said "Yes!" It was the best decision I ever made.

When we returned to Tommy's van, I mentioned how it would have been nice to have my father's blessings for us to get married, along with Mom's. My dad had passed away a few years prior, and Tommy got to know him before God's Angels came to take him to his heavenly home and relieve his suffering from Parkinson's disease.

Suddenly, several brightly colored Monarch butterflies appeared out of nowhere and flew around the windshield of the van. Was this a message sent from my father to let us know of his approval?

Well, my curiosity got to me, so I did some research on Monarch butterflies and learned that they migrate from Canada and fly as far as California. My father, who was born in Maine but raised in Canada, married my mother, who was also from Canada, and they moved to the United States. Dad fought in the Canadian army and traveled to many places, although I do not know if he set foot in California. Regardless, if this truly was a message from him, he would know that these beautiful butterflies would spark my interest and curiosity, and I would question why they came flying around Tommy's van out of nowhere. He knew that I would research it and eventually make a connection. The word Canada stood out, which gave it away.

Photo: Monarch butterfly, 2001.

Photo: Starr Rae's father

My Near-Death Experience and Devotion to Saint Michael

O N SEPTEMBER 25, 2006, I became very ill. We thought it was from food poisoning, so Tommy drove me to an urgent care center. Shortly after being examined, I was rushed to the hospital after my blood work showed a high white blood cell count. After going through a series of tests, they determined that a hard fecalith mass (compacted fecal matter) was lodged inside my appendix. The doctor was adamant about scheduling surgery as soon as possible, but I was a wuss (and am still not the least bit ashamed to admit it.)

When it came to serious medical intervention, I was not the most compliant patient to deal with, especially when it came to granting permission to an unknown doctor to perform surgery on me. I had high hopes of just passing the damned thing overnight, so I stayed in bed as recommended and prayed to God and every saint I could think of to intercede and relieve me of the dreadful affliction.

Around 3:00 a.m., I started to go into convulsions. I kept pressing the nurse's call button but could barely speak due to violent shivering and uncontrollable teeth chattering. It felt like I was inside an ice chamber, on the verge of freezing to death, and I have to admit I was glad the doctor would not let me go home. The pain, which had gone away earlier, came back, and it felt a million times worse. I was eager to consent to surgery. In fact, I would have done the surgery on myself at that point. My appendix had ruptured, causing my body to become dangerously septic from E. coli, and peritonitis. Then, I had an inexplicable experience. We were told that, down the road, I may have had a near-death experience.

It was nothing like the stories we hear about, there was no white light or tunnel. I was seated in a reclining position, inside a room, and sensed a protective presence staying by my side during some sort of a trial before a dark, shadowy image that attempted to obtain sinful and evil thoughts from me. Uncanny as it was, fear was not part of my experience, only the feeling of peace and safety, as I felt guarded by my defender. Although it was not seen or heard, this ally provided me ample strength and courage to face the dark image and speak out loud with conviction, "You will never get my soul, because Jesus Christ is my Lord and Savior!"

After I was rushed into surgery, then began the process of a slow recovery, I tried to forget about the weird experience. One day, I confided to a friend about the strange encounter. She told me that Saint Michael the Archangel is known to assist and fight for dying souls and protects them from Satan's attacks. In the bible, Satan is known as "The Accuser." He accuses us of our sins before God and wants us to bear the weight of its shame, to feel unworthy of God's forgiveness and grace. The trial I had undergone during my experience seemed to resonate with what she said. "

"Now have salvation and power come, and the kingdom of our God and the authority of His anointed. For the accuser of our brothers is cast out, who accuses them before our God day and night." (Revelation 12:10) (NABRE)

She showed me a photo of Saint Michael holding a sword in his hand. Tommy and I had both competed as collegiate fencers and were active in seventeenth-century swordsmanship groups for many years. We held swords and various weapons in ours hands all the time. We recalled the surgeon telling us how lucky I was to pull through the surgery, it was a very close call.

I had angelic experiences prior to this one, but none as intense. We did not know much about Saint Michael, but as time went on, we found out that he would educate us.

One night during a seventeenth-century fencing practice, Saint Michael made his presence known. My bizarre experience had been tucked away, and I started to doubt it even happened. However, that evening something took over my physical body and earned me a weapon authorization while landing perfect kill shots against one of the best teachers, who had been fencing a heck of a lot longer than I had. It was great not to be on the skewered end for a change! Then, my pride kicked in, *Wahoo!! I am really kicking the teacher's butt tonight!*

Suddenly, I had a flashback to my experience in the hospital, and a voice spoke to my heart, "It was I who was with you that night of fate, and I who fought for your soul! You need to witness now!" There was a good possibility I went into shock and nearly dropped my sword and dagger to the floor. All at once, I felt the aftershock of my countless attempts in the past, trying to earn these weapon authorizations. It was grueling after having my surgeries, from not being fast enough. My great-grandmother could have kicked my butt blindfolded if she was still alive. But that night, the teacher could barely parry against my attacks. Everything felt surrealistic.

Was this a dream?

Then I heard the teachers call out my name. They actually gave me a dagger authorization, something out of the ordinary, because an authorization has to be requested, then earned. Normally, the requester had to go through a rigorous armor inspection first, before the marshals scrutinized your ability, as you fought your best against an opponent. Afterward, they would decide if you were skilled enough to earn the authorization.

That night, Saint Michael the Archangel would not allow me to feel defeated again. He helped me win an authorization but, more importantly, he won my heart and devotion. From that moment on, his strong presence, comfort, and guidance were felt in my life. It is amazing how God works to get your attention!

Pictures of Saint Michael usually depict him holding a sword in one hand, as a defeated Satan lies helpless at his feet. For many years, Tommy and I had held many different types of swords such as foils, sabers, epees, and rapiers. We also used other weapons when we practiced seventeenth-century swordsmanship, including daggers and bucklers. We never made the connection, until one evening at a fencing practice, and our lives were forever changed. The time had come to start giving witness.

Quis Ut Deus! Who is like God?!" The mighty war cry of Saint Michael!

Photo: (left) Starr Rae and (right) Tommy fencing at
a seventeenth-century rapier demonstration.

Photo: (left) Tommy and (right) Starr Rae during an electronic epee bout.

Photo: (left) Starr Rae and (right) Tommy as spectators view their seventeenth-century rapier demonstration. The Annual Polish American Festival at The National Shrine of Our Lady of Czestochowa, Doylestown, Pennsylvania. Used with permission.

Photo: Tommy and Starr Rae at The New York Renaissance Faire. Circa 2011. Used with permission.

My emergency appendectomy, on September 26, 2006, was three days before The Feast of Saint Michael and the Archangels (Michaelmas), which is celebrated September 29. What we found to be really thought provoking, however, was that 350 years ago, around September 26, 1656, there was a plague at Gargano, Italy, near the Cave of Saint Michael. It has been said that the Bishop prayed to God for Saint Michael's intercession to rescue the small town from the scourge. The mighty angel appeared and ordered the Bishop to bless and use the stones of the grotto to save the town from the affliction. The Bishop obeyed the command, and the plague left the area. It is remarkable how this miraculous event happened close to or possibly on the exact date of my emergency appendectomy, 350 years earlier. The incredible experience I had makes it more meaningful. Feeling grateful and blessed to still be alive, and given a second chance, it is with great joy I will be able to share with you some of my stories, which I refer to as my angelic experiences.

Photo: Starr Rae a few weeks after her surgery with the statue of Saint Michael located on the campus of The National Centre for Padre Pio, Inc. Barto, Pennsylvania. Used with permission.

Looking Back with Some Help from Saint Michael

S EVERAL YEARS AFTER my appendix ruptured, we reflected on the near-fatal night and what the heck happened. Catholics are taught that Heaven, Purgatory, and Hell exist, so some questions came to mind. *Was one of those places lined up for me, awaiting my arrival? Did God let me live and give me another chance to get things right? Did he let me live to talk, or rather write, about it?* I do not think I am or ever was an evil person. A sinner? Undeniably, yes, but my intentions have always been good. I try to be the person God created me to be.

Could it be that in His eyes I have been evil without being aware of it? Evil in the sense of not surrendering my life completely to His will, by not being the Christian witness He wants me to be? I was really trying to do my best, and still am, but I still make mistakes. I often wonder how anyone could live without a close relationship with God. The one true joy that I really felt, deep in my soul, was upon my return to His Holy Church, to seek his friendship, guidance, and love.

Satan was not content. He successfully guided me away from praying and attending Mass to worship God with His community of believers, like he does to so many others with his cunning lies and deceit.

We sometimes turn away from God and His Holy Church. Why? Because people, including priests, say and do things that we do not like. Other people's stupid or sinful actions can seriously jeopardize our relationship with God because of this. We forget we all fall short and need God's help to get us back on the right path again. The Church is God's House of Worship and offers healing for all of us sinners. Turning our backs on our creator can allow the prince of darkness to guide us away. He can even convince us to stop praying! Now I can see so clearly how my emergency surgery actually came as a blessing. It was time to wake up and smell the incense.

I will never forget what happened in my hospital room that night. I almost died! Yet, here I am, past survivor, present warrior, and able to talk about it. Something or someone was there to protect me. Saint Michael, I truly believe, shields, fights for, and rescues our souls from Satan's accusations when we die.

Many years ago, before my appendix burst and I developed peritonitis myself, one of our beloved pets got terminally sick from peritonitis. She was given a 5 percent chance to live, yet she survived a daunting surgery and blood transfusion. The surgeon said it was a miracle she pulled through. I developed a strong devotion to Saint Francis of Assisi as we prayed for his intercession to God to heal her. Saint Francis also played an important role in returning me back to my faith, which was strengthened years later when I came close to death myself.

For the longest time, while praying the Saint Michael prayer, a huge lump formed in my throat. All of these occurrences involving God's Holy Angels in my life during the past several years have led me to believe beyond the shadow of a doubt that they exist. There is too much going on here. How can all of this just be coincidence? God sends His Holy messengers to help us fulfill our destinies while on earth, and to defend us from that SOB we call Satan. *But God, why do these experiences happen to me? Why me?* I am not of a high intellect, scholarly, or one influential or eloquent in speech. At times, these experiences can be met with much reproach.

People out there, perhaps even you, reading this right now, might even think I am one beer short of a six-pack. Well, the truth is these experiences are available to everyone. You do not have to be special. They are available to anyone with faith and open to receiving God's graces. In time, you will become more aware of the presence of God's Holy Angels in your own life. My husband, now a believer, has seen enough to be convinced.

Have you ever questioned why God allows all the suffering we go through in life? Why is there so much of it, and why? Could this be His way of sanctifying our souls and sending us wisdom through our life experiences? We do tend to turn back when we hit rock bottom. There is no other way but up, and when we finally resurface, we are able to see more clearly, with a better understanding of how everything does work out for the greater good.

These events tend to eventually bring us closer to God. It is easier to look back and see how things turned out for the best instead of trying to see what lies ahead. Trials and hardships in time teach us that we cannot get through our struggles alone without God's help, no matter how hard we try. He pushes us to become better people by permitting Satan to send hardships and challenges to test our faith. God's glory is then revealed when we become transformed into mature, more loving, and compassionate people.

After an immune-system disorder and three major surgeries within a year, I contracted chronic late-stage Lyme disease, was treated twice, and was told only 20 percent of patients make a complete recovery. I continue to fight some post-Lyme disease complications, along with migraines, but believe these afflictions made me more sensitive and empathetic toward the suffering of my brothers and sisters.

Although physical setbacks can cause exhausting efforts to combat and transform them, much more can be gained in our spiritual strength if we trust God, surrender our wills to His, and allow Him to be the guiding force in our lives. He will bring light upon His miracles at work when we are open to receiving His graces. Then we can feel the love He wants to send our way.

My entire life transformed before my eyes into nothing less of a miracle. My own suffering and trials led me to become more patient (sometimes!), to have more trust, and to develop a stronger faith in God.

"For He commands His Angels with regard to you, to guard you wherever you go. With their hands they shall support you, lest you strike your foot against a stone." (Psalm 91:11–12) (NABRE).

God's plans turned out for the greater good after all, eventually leading me on this incredible path, and here I am writing about it! What a tremendous blessing it has been for me to have a wonderful husband by my side, who never runs short of laughter and puts a smile on my face, especially when it's most needed. Growing in our faith together, we mutually agree that, so far, this has been one heck of an amazing journey for both of us!

Photo: Angel of the Guard. Antonio de Pereda. 1646. Public Domain.

My Mother's Remarkable Hospital Experience

WE WILL NEVER forget the experience my mother had after her second resection from colon cancer in late 2006. It happened while she still resided in her home in New Jersey. At that time, I developed an incisional hernia during the recovery from my emergency appendectomy, and gallstones took up residence inside my gallbladder, which needed to be evicted. Surgery was necessary, however it would have to be delayed a year, as Mom's cancer fight was top priority. We planned to get her through her surgery and rehab before I had my own surgery. Tommy and I traveled back and forth from Pennsylvania to visit with her every day, excluding nights when we slept at her house.

As time went on, my hernia got larger, and laparoscopic surgery was no longer an option. Luckily, I felt no pain until after we got my mother through her surgery and rehab and it was time for me to have the surgery.

While Mom was in the hospital recuperating from her surgery, she shared a room with a woman who moaned a lot. The woman received company during visiting hours, but barely spoke, so Mom chatted with her visitors as they sat next to the woman's bed and found out they were the woman's adult children. A curtain between their beds was drawn in the evening and the woman's moaning continued through the night, which kept my mother awake. Finally, she requested to be moved into another room.

That same night, the curtain was drawn as usual. Around midnight, Mom heard the woman start to moan. This time the woman also made strange noises Mom never heard before. Mom called out to her, asking if she was in pain, then looked over at the curtain towards her. A dark image was hovering over the woman's bed, transparent in appearance. The woman immediately responded in a loud, frightening, guttural voice, "My pain is with God!"

The rest of the evening, my poor mother just laid there, terrified. No sleep came and she was wide awake, so frightened that all she could do was pray for the safety of the woman and herself.

The following day, the woman's visitors returned, and the woman began to moan again. Something prompted my mother to ask, "This is none of my business, but is your mother Catholic?"

Photo: Saint Anthony Attacked by Devils. Limbourg brothers. 1408. Public Domain.

They replied, "Yes."

Mom suggested, "Maybe she should see a priest?" They took mom's advice and went to the nurse's station to put in a request for a priest to see their mother. Miraculously, a priest arrived within minutes, went over to the woman's bed, prayed over her, heard her confession, performed The Prayer of Absolution, administered Holy Communion, then exited the room.

Five minutes later, the woman died. My mother witnessed it all.

Did a divine intervention take place? Was Mom provoked to help save this poor woman's suffering soul? Perhaps it was more than that.

After the deceased woman was taken from the room, one of her sons came over to Mom's bed and said, "Thank you. I will never forget you, or what happened here."

A few weeks later, I accompanied Mom to her doctor's office for her follow-up visit. He apologized for the noisy roommate in the hospital. Mom told him about the woman's moaning and the weird guttural sounds that she heard one evening. He confirmed her story and told us he heard the same sounds also as he entered the room to check on Mom, and expressed how frightening they were, even as a doctor who had seen and heard a lot of strange things during his practice.

He said what she heard was not imagined, was not a side effect from medication or lack of sleep, and it was one heck of a scary ordeal for a woman her age to have gone through, especially after just surviving a huge surgery.

My mother must have been petrified. Although she was a tough cookie, she was also a faith-filled woman who placed her trust in God, and must have prayed the entire night, which helped her survive it.

After driving Mom home from her appointment and visiting for a while, I started the drive back home. Merging onto the highway, questions began to pop into my head: Was this for real? Maybe they both imagined it. The experience was bizarre to say the least. The thought of Satan arose: Does he really exist? Is he really the red man depicted with horns on his head, wielding a pitchfork? Was this something made up as a scare tactic to keep us all in line, or just stuff from our overactive imaginations?

The answers and the truth were already known, as I had witnessed it myself. My near-death experience provided substantial proof of the evil one's presence. Mom was not the only one who observed that menacing, dark image. All of those questions put into my mind were a temptation from Satan, trying to convince me that he does not exist.

Of course, the red man with horns and a pitchfork are human imagination. What he looks like remains a mystery. I recalled reading somewhere that once he was God's most beautiful angel before his pride took over and he became wicked.

To clear my mind of these thoughts, I turned on the radio and sang along with the song on the air. Shortly after, a white box van came up fast behind me out of nowhere. As it passed, I noticed it was a company van with an extremely eye-catching logo, a huge devil's face with two massive horns.

Our Saint Michael Statue

A STRONG FEELING CAME over me one morning to go to one of our local Christian bookstores. Many interesting statues and plaques greeted me upon entering the store and something caught the corner of my eye. Looking down, next to my feet was a statue of Saint Michael. I searched for a price tag, but there was none to be found. We had admired garden statues in other people's yards, but never really considered getting one. But today was different. This statue was special. The saleslady noticed my interest and stated that the statue was defective and not for sale. My heart sunk. A tiny voice inside persuaded me, "Ask her to consult the manager about it."

Photo: Our Saint Michael statue at nighttime.

Upon her return, she announced the manager would sell it to me for $10.00.

"Sold!" I shouted enthusiastically!

The statue of Saint Michael was waiting to be rescued by me, and I scored it for ten bucks! The only thing wrong was that the base was slightly nicked. It felt like I hit the mother lode. I called Tommy on my cell phone from inside the car. "Honey, you will never believe who is in the trunk of our car!"

There was nothing but dead silence. He must have thought I had finally lost it. A sigh of relief came from him after he heard the story.

Saint Michael's new home is now on our front porch. His spot-light casts a shadow on the wall behind him, which emphasizes his wings. You can see them clearly, even from the street. It is a constant reminder that he watches over us and our neighborhood.

The Salad Bar Angels

O NE AFTERNOON WHILE mulling around at the supermarket, I accidentally dropped my cell phone and didn't realize it. At the checkout, I thought I heard my name being paged at customer service.

Is it my imagination, or am I hearing things? Who would be paging me in the middle of the day when everyone we know is at work?

Having not slept well for the past couple of days, I wondered if it was just a hallucination. Looking around to see if one of our friends was in the store playing tricks on me, I saw no one in sight and figured it was from my run-down condition.

The checkout line moved, and it was time to pay for my groceries. Reaching into my handbag, I opened my wallet, pulled out my credit card, and noticed my cell phone was missing! Maybe what I heard was real and their customer service knew something I didn't? After paying the bill, I sprinted over to the service counter. They had paged me indeed, because someone found my cell phone and was honest enough to turn it in.

How did a perfect stranger know who to have paged? How did they know my name? This was an older flip phone, without all the bells and whistles we have access to nowadays. My name was not on it.

After unloading the groceries at home, a message appeared on our home phone from our friend April, telling us that she tried to call me on my cell phone in the afternoon and a woman she did not know answered it. Apparently, April had tried to call while I was shopping at the supermarket. Luckily, a stranger heard my phone ringing, and was surprised to find it in the salad bar. She decided to answer it to find out who it belonged to and told April she would drop it off at the service desk, so they would know whose name to page. Obviously, I had dropped it while I was getting my lunch. April must have been totally confused as to who this woman was who was answering my phone.

Can you imagine finding a cell phone inside a salad bar? I do not know about you, but to me, it would not be very appetizing, especially finding it in the lettuce bin! That poor woman more than likely went straight to customer service, then went somewhere else to eat, or maybe she just skipped lunch altogether! It is consoling to know there are still honest people out there.

Fortunately, the good angels knew this woman was one of them and picked her out, knowing she would return my phone and even catch me while I was still in the store. Hopefully, she received a blessing from them for being such a Good Samaritan. A huge thank you went out to my Earth angel friend April and the Holy Angels for rescuing my phone and saving me a trip back to the supermarket.

Photo: Angel holding olive branch.
Hans Memling. 1475-1480.
Public Domain.

Angel from India

S URE, WITH ALL of the people down here on Earth, the angels must be very busy, but if you are open to them you will receive many great opportunities to see them at work in your life. This can be through events, people, or even the smallest of miraculous happenings.

New sneakers were on my list of needed items, so Tommy and I went shopping. The parking lot was jammed, but the good angels provided a front-row parking spot. Within minutes of entering the store, a well-fitted and -priced pair of sneakers were found, plus five Christmas gifts for friends and family. Certain items were priced at 50 percent off, plus we got an additional 15 percent off with a coupon. We were pressed for time, but everything was done in the record-breaking time of one hour, and we were out the door with an additional fifteen minutes to spare. It was a pleasant drive back home, without much traffic.

Later in the evening, we arranged to meet up with our new friend Ashithra, who we met at one of our church's functions. Her job relocated her to our area from India, and she was staying at a local extended-stay hotel. She was only twenty-six years old and felt homesick and very much alone in a strange country, since she only knew a few of her coworkers. Guardian appeared on our caller ID whenever she called. Imagine how this name popping up on our phone sparked my interest!

We took her shopping, and she was very excited looking at the merchandise because the store was beautifully decorated for the approaching Christmas season. She told us she had never seen snow, so we promised to help her build her first snowman if it snowed enough to make one.

Through Divine Intervention, God's Holy Angels brought us together and the three of us became close friends immediately. Tommy and I learned so much about her culture and family life. She even showed me how to correctly wear a beautiful sari. We attended many fun events together, including a local Renaissance Christmas concert. She was very excited when I loaned her some of my period clothing so we could step out in style together. She looked fabulous dressed up in my tunic and side-less surcoat. Spending the holidays with her was such a joy and a blessing. We enjoyed each other's company tremendously.

In the four short months she was here, we had many wonderful times together. We all felt very sad when the day came to say goodbye, as she had to fly back home. Her husband came to visit while she was here, and we had the pleasure of meeting him. The laughter and memories will last forever, and we have developed an enduring friendship with them.

God likes to place certain people in our path. He likes to place angels unawares.

Photo: (left) Ashithra and (right) Starr Rae.
Used with permission.

Shopping with the Angels

T HE THOUGHT THAT God never allows you to outdo him in good deeds or generosity has gone through my mind several times during my life. It seems that whenever a good deed is done without telling anyone or being noticed, he gives back something. His rewards are plentiful, and easy to spot if you just watch for them, acknowledge them, and then offer thanks to Him whenever they present themselves. Some may be quite evident, while others are more subtle.

Once I found a beautiful wreath on sale and purchased it for only $5.00. It was a perfect match to our home decor. Needing new clothes and shopping for them can be a challenging task for me. Often nothing fits, or the selection is not appealing. It is tough when you prefer younger styles and would like to dress more like a woman in her thirties, but you are pushing higher digits. Drawstring pants have worked best for me all these years after going through some daunting surgeries. The majority of jeans that I like are mostly for thinner, younger women, or those who do not have a husband who considers multiple ice cream cartons a staple in their freezer. When I try on those hip hugger-style jeans, within minutes I am trying to prevent them from sliding down my hips to avoid sporting that pants-to-the-ground look.

Ladies who are pushing those higher digits with me, do not forget about those clearance racks! If you are in the right place at the right time, they can provide you with some nice items at a terrific price without sacrificing or cramping your style. Ask God's Holy Angels for help, and they will assist you!

One particular day, it seemed like the salesgirls were putting out clothing faster than I could try it on. Feeling pretty darned elated, a few items were thrown into my basket. *Wahoo! This is going to be a good day! Should I trade the basket for a cart?* Then something caught my eye. A gorgeous, much-needed bathing suit with a marked-down price tag beckoned me back to the racks, then to the fitting room.

Later that evening, our neighbor's daughter was taking in her mother's mail across the street. We went over to talk, and she told us her mom was in the hospital, having surgery on her foot, after she had fallen. We promised to pray for her mother to have a quick and painless recovery.

When Tommy and I crossed the street, we walked up the path leading to the front door and the spotlight lit up our Saint Michael statue. The light has a timer, and it was scheduled to turn on around 10:00 p.m., but it came on at 9:00 p.m. that evening. Was Saint Michael telling us that he overheard the conversation between us and our neighbor's daughter over her mother's injury and he wanted us to know he would be watching over her and protecting her during her stay in the hospital?

"Give to the Most High as he has given to you, generously, according to your means. For he is a God who always repays and will give back to you sevenfold." (Sirach 35:12). (NABRE).

Photo: Christ in Limbo. Fra Angelico.
1450. Public Domain.

My Mother's Move

T HE DAY WE moved my mother from her house in New Jersey into an apartment closer to where Tommy and I live in Pennsylvania was very stressful. It almost felt like the good angels abandoned us on the journey. The spotlight on Saint Michael's statue was on the blink and it seemed like there was not much, if any, positive angelic activity going on.

My Chaplet of Saint Michael CD had been missing for weeks. A little voice inside told me to search the car again, despite the fact we had searched it together a few times and had not found it. This time, it was in the door panel. Perfect timing. We listened to it on the way to Mom's house, praying that her choice to move closer to us would have a positive impact on us all. Although it was rush hour on our way back home, there was not much traffic.

At her apartment, the movers began bringing her furniture inside and a minor earthquake struck! It was strange that Mom felt it while she was sitting on her reclining chair, but Tommy and I, sitting next to her on her couch did not feel a thing.

When everything was finished being moved and situated, we took Mom out and treated her to dinner. It was a pleasant surprise when our waitress told us our food took too long to be prepared and served, so it was free of charge! Saint Michael alerted us to his presence and was still at work. His day was still not quite over yet.

Mom stayed overnight at our house that evening, and before bedtime she sat in the living room with us, looking through one of my favorite books. On the cover was a picture of Saint Michael. She expressed an interest to read it, so we gave her a copy of it to keep. She seemed relaxed and content. We reflected on the events of the day, then thanked God, His Angels, and Saint Michael for all the blessings we had received.

Tommy and I, plus many other friends, including those in the intercessory prayer group, would pray that, God willing, my mother would not take long to root herself. All that was needed was for her to make a connection with her unaccustomed surroundings, settle into her lovely apartment, and make some friends. Luckily, my mother was not a person who would give way to living a solitary life and avoid others. A very social woman, more than likely she would not spend too much time sitting around in her apartment. She loved to walk and be outside in nature. Perhaps she would fall in love, like Tommy and I did, with her beautiful new home state.

Would you believe that five days after we moved my mother into her new apartment, Hurricane Irene came through? Everyone who heard the story got a good laugh when we told them my mother's move to Pennsylvania actually triggered an earthquake, then a few days later, a hurricane. Even Mom found it funny. We joked about it for years.

Photo: Angels in Adoration. Benozzo Gozzoli.
1459. Public Domain.

Downtown Angel Signs

W HILE WALKING DOWNTOWN one afternoon, my mind raced over what seemed like an endless list of things that needed to get done. Momentarily, my mental to-do list was hushed by the thought of a vacation and how much Tommy and I needed one. I could see chalk on the sidewalk ahead, where something was written in big letters. "Vote for Vacation!" The angels seemed to agree with me, confirming it in those big, bright colors.

A few weeks went by, and we were deeply concerned about my mother, who was not acclimating well to her apartment, the area, and her new lifestyle. The stress was taking a toll on us. Our physical, mental, and emotional health was going completely haywire. Tommy and I kept reassuring each other that eventually Mom would settle, get involved in some groups, and maybe even join a Bible study. Hopefully, she would be grateful for no longer having the responsibility of maintaining a house or all the yard work that needed to be done, and become familiar with shopping in the nearby supermarket that she told us she felt lost in. There were also many nice convenient stores besides it, within walking distance from her apartment, which made it a perfect location for her because she loved to walk.

Where my mother had chosen to live could not have been a nicer place. Her apartment was lovely, warm, and welcoming. The tenants who lived there were very friendly, and there was an assortment of wonderful things to do nearby, but she was unhappy regardless. It would take time to get her rooted, but it was taking longer than we thought it would.

I walked past a jewelry store with a sign in the window. It said, "Free Head Exams."

Are God's Holy Angels suggesting I get my head examined or that we should all get our heads examined? Should it be done before or after the vacation that was just voted for?

Finding this quite comical, I actually laughed out loud.

Our smoke detector started making peeping sounds that evening. I was wearing a purple marshmallow Peeps shirt and, pointing down to the image of the yellow, sugary confection, made a silly comment and Tommy laughed. We can be really silly sometimes, known to laugh our heads off over complete nonsense, especially if we are stressed or overtired. Knowing that laughter is healthy and a wonderful way to relieve tension, there have been many times when we laughed so hard I got tears in my eyes and could hardly breathe, causing me to make bizarre squeaky noises in the back of my throat, which made us laugh even harder. At times, we can even forget what we are laughing about in the first place. Do you ever wonder if God and His Holy Angels have a sense of humor and laugh along with us, or do they think we are just a bunch of nincompoops?

Photo: With Love. A message from Starr Rae to the angels.

Electronics and Angels

A LL OF A sudden, I heard the sound of music, which seemed to be streaming from our bedroom. Walking into the room to see where the music was coming from, I realized that it was emanating from the radio/alarm clock on my nightstand, next to our bed. I must have accidentally hit the snooze button when I woke up, setting the alarm to go off at a later time.

Upon examination, however, both the radio and alarm clock were in the off position. Somehow the music was blaring, and it would not shut off!

After a while, though, it just stopped on its own. When Tommy arrived home from work, he checked it and said he could not find anything wrong with it. The night before, he woke up early in the morning and noticed that our space heater was on. He questioned if I turned it back on. I replied, "Of course not." We were certain it was turned off before going to sleep, because we had a lengthy discussion about the safety of keeping it on overnight. The fear of fire or waking up hot and sweaty was a valid enough reason to turn it off. We had mutually agreed upon it. There was no explanation for how it got turned on. Was this just another fluky circumstance?

Photo: Our small space heater.

A Brown, Furry-Tailed Angel

W HILE TALKING ON the phone with my friend Linda, I happened to glance through our dining room window to see our resident groundhog, Ethelred, run across the snow from our neighbor's backyard behind us and into our backyard. She was racing back and forth in our rock garden like the devil was chasing after her. It was an odd sight in the late morning during the dead of winter, when it was windy and very cold outside with snow on the ground.

I asked Linda, "What is this crazy groundhog doing out in this cold weather, running back and forth. Isn't she supposed to be in hibernation?"

Linda responded, "Maybe she's having a hot flash?"

We both laughed. All of a sudden, Ethelred stopped short, stood up on her hind legs, and looked directly at me. I quizzically stared back at her through the window. Back down she went, into her hole, only to stick her head right back out to look at me again, then she walked over to one of our plants. *Was she hungry and intending to take a bite out of it? Maybe she was hungry, but why would she go after a frozen plant? What in the world is going on inside this crazy whistle pig's head?*

Now she had my full attention. Banging on the glass, I loudly reprimanded her, but she continued to run back and forth across the rock garden. It seemed like she was trying to desperately get my attention. Trying to ignore it, I continued talking to Linda, while periodically yelling at the groundhog. Finally fed up from the interruptions, Linda decided we should hang up, and told me to go investigate what was happening in our backyard.

Believe it or not, this groundhog is not the typical destructive woodchuck most people complain about. She is pretty smart and seems to be aware of the boundaries of what she is allowed and not allowed to do if she wants to continue living here. She often pokes her head out of her hole when we whistle, listens to us talk, and hangs out on her rock sunning herself, especially when Tommy is playing his guitar, I am playing my bass, or if the radio is on. She also comes out of her hole and listens when we do karaoke. We have come to accept and love her, as she has never been a problem and is a real sweetie that can be quite comical and entertaining to watch at times.

I threw my coat on and went out into our backyard to see what the matter was.

A strange noise sounded like it was coming from the back of our house. Much to my dismay, our garden hose had sprung a leak and water was spraying all over our patio, leaving me no choice but to run as fast as possible to turn off the faucet that was accidentally left on. It rendered me drenched and freezing, far from being in a good mood.

Our smart little groundhog was trying to warn us about the leaky hose! She saved us from an expensive water bill and maybe even a flooded yard. Could there be a possibility that some of God's Earth Angels have brown furry tails?

Photo: Ethelred the groundhog.

God Answers in Mysterious Ways

T WO JOGGERS WERE several yards behind me one day during my daily walk around our neighborhood. Staying to the left of the road so they could pass me easily, I immediately turned back to look at them, and they were gone. This was strange. If they went to one of the houses, or headed to the other end of the block, I would have seen them. I let go of the thought and continued my walk while thanking the Lord for the beautiful day, the miracles He sent into my life the past couple of years, the many blessings, and for the ability to walk while enjoying His beautiful creation.

Squirrels ran past me while birds flew overhead singing their songs and it inspired me to reflect on how much love I have for animals, which is close, if not equal, to my love for humans. Perhaps being born on the Feast of Saint Francis of Assisi had a huge influence on me. I always felt a strong connection to all of God's creatures. At the time this story took place, it had been thirty-five years since I decided to become a vegetarian. How long and lonely a path it was, and I traveled it alone most of my life. Even as a young child, I remembered questioning my parents why people ate dead animals, and the question lasted well into adulthood. Eventually, at the age of twenty, my parent's dietary lifestyle became something I could no longer live by or even try to comprehend, so I walked away from eating meat. The thought of animals being slaughtered mercilessly, especially when there were other options for survival caused me great anguish, and I knew it would never be the way for me to live in peace. I love all the animals God has created and could not bear the thought of any single one of them suffering.

The conviction cast me up against the beliefs of generations. Often the subject triggered interrogations, leaving me feeling persecuted or rejected for being different and not conforming to the opinions of the vast majority. *God, have I been wrong to extend mercy to all of your creatures, not just to us humans and those animals considered as pets? To stand against violence and cruelty, to seek an alternative way of survival?* A deep distress filled my soul. Perhaps I was wrong all this time, and everyone against my vegetarian lifestyle was right?

Thoughts shifted to my narrow escape from death, and my battle against Lyme Disease, which targeted me twice. The Lyme support group revealed how awful this disease can be, as it leaves many incapacitated. Yet, miraculously, there I was, walking a mile, sometimes more, a couple of days a week, then eventually being able to ride a bicycle several miles. In the beginning, it was difficult to walk. My gait was off, and I got winded within a few minutes and felt pain all over my body, especially in my joints. It was only through the Grace of God that I was able to work through it and not give up.

On damp and cold days, I still force myself to walk to relieve the stiffness and pain, sometimes bundled up in single-digit weather, however I have come a long distance and believe my healthy, plant-based diet is what has mostly healed me, plus having a positive attitude and firm faith in God to give me the determination to pull through.

"I will restore you to health; of your wounds I will heal you," says the Lord. From them will resound songs of praise, the laughter of happy men. I will make them not few, but many; they will not be tiny, for I will glorify them." (Jeremiah 30:17a, 19) (NAB)

A survivor can become a warrior if they trust God and set their mind to it. God did not want me yet. He wanted me to stick around for reasons unknown.

Turning the corner, my walk picked up at a quicker pace. Up the street, in the distance, was a ball of fur against a curb. The feeling of dread rushed upon me over the possibility of it being a wounded or dead animal. God places me in these situations from time to time, knowing there will be an intervention with a rescue or burial if necessary. The rescues are handled fine, it's the severely wounded animals or dead ones that cause me a great deal of anxiety. At that point, a call is made to my wildlife-rescue contact and she comes to take over.

With much relief, I discovered it was just a cute little stuffed animal that looked like a hedgehog or a groundhog. It made me think about our resident groundhog Ethelred. My heart felt much lighter when a quote from the Bible entered my mind. God must have heard my question and he answered it.

Photo: A cute little stuffed animal.

"Use the faith you have as your rule of life in the sight of the Lord. Happy the man whose conscience does not condemn what he has chosen to do. But if a man eats when his conscience has misgivings about eating, he is already condemned, because he is not acting in accordance with what he believes." (Romans 14:22–23) (NAB).

If love rules your heart and your intentions are pure despite what others may think, and their opinions are contrary to yours, you will never fail to do what is right in The Lord's eyes.

I offered a prayer for the child who may have lost their furry little friend and asked God to return it to them and to send them comfort, a feeling similar to what He just sent my way. I started to head back home. *What about those joggers who disappeared at the beginning of my walk?* Again, the whisper entered my heart: Don't worry about them, they got your back.

Hurricane Sandy Angels

A s Hurricane Sandy wreaked havoc on the East Coast October 29, 2012, none of us imagined things would turn out the way they did. On that blustery evening, around 8:30 p.m., we looked from our dining room window to see the huge row of pine trees in our backyard whipping back and forth from the strong winds. We could not help but feel apprehensive that one or more of those trees might come down upon our house. A strong feeling came upon me to ask God to send Saint Michael and His Holy Angels for our protection. I asked Tommy to pray with me and we sat on the couch. Holding hands, we prayed for all of our neighbors as well. A gut feeling told me to prepare, as something terrible was about to happen.

Around 8:45 p.m., we heard five very loud booms. Transformers were exploding in our neighborhood, followed by pink and purple lights in the sky. I questioned Tommy about the lights, and he thought they may have been caused by an oncoming thunder and lightning storm, as we did not know yet about the transformers. One of them exploded along the back of our neighbor Rita's house. It fell to the ground, starting a small fire, causing a power outage on the rest of our street. Soon after, a few fire trucks arrived in front of her house. From our guest room window, through the darkness, we could observe the silhouette of a tree, a huge tree, which appeared to be lying over the roof of her house.

I put my coat on and headed next door to check on Rita and was stunned to discover that a huge sycamore tree had fallen on the roof of her house. It extended from her back yard, across the middle of her roof, to the walkway and entrance to her front door. We were shocked to find out the branches actually speared through the roof and were inside her house, reaching almost as far down as the basement! The roof, kitchen, and dining room were completely destroyed, along with her sunroom, on which a renovation had just been finished the day before.

It was like stumbling upon a really scary action-packed movie set or having a terrible dream. Several firemen were standing in her front yard, yelling at all of the curious neighbors who had gathered to see what happened. "Please, stay away! This is very dangerous!"

Fortunately, Rita and her dog, Ralph, were not harmed. An urgent feeling had come over her to go to bed earlier, instead of staying up later to watch TV. Ralph followed her to the bedroom around 8:30 p.m., and they settled for the night.

It was around 8:45, when the transformers exploded and we lost power, that the heavy winds caused the tree in her backyard to fall and crash through the roof where she and Ralph would have been together watching TV had they not gone to bed. They would have been killed.

The tree destroyed everything in its path. Amazingly, no damage was in the bedroom where they went to sleep. The tree fell fifteen minutes after Tommy and I prayed for protection, pulling down several wires from the telephone pole next to her house, along with the enflamed transformer. It was a miracle the power went out, as those wires that landed on top of her house could have caused a deadly fire. Our house, next door, would have been next.

Although she was in a state of shock, Rita and Ralph managed to get out of the house safely and unharmed, thanks to the firemen who arrived and bravely ventured inside her house to rescue them. A few days later, Rita told us about the apprehension she experienced around 8:30, then the urge to leave the living room to go to bed. Luckily, she responded to the warning and they were able to escape from the impending danger before it happened.

A few of us got together with Rita afterward to talk about the events that unfolded before our eyes that disastrous evening. All who witnessed it firmly believe God heard our prayers and sent His Holy Warrior Angels to guard us and all of our neighbors, especially Rita and her dog. Our house was the only one on our side of the block without any downed trees or damage.

Photo: The damage done to Rita's house the day after Hurricane Sandy struck.
Used with permission. 2012.

A Message to Comfort

E XTREME WIND AND heavy, pouring rain kept me awake late one
night as my husband and I were snuggled together in bed. The
neighborhood was still trying to recover from the major impact of
Hurricane Sandy and the terrible damage it had done to our neighbor Rita's home a few months ago. On edge about the pine trees in our
backyard, I pictured them the same way they looked the evening the
hurricane struck. It was not going to be a restful night, at least for me.

Tommy had already fallen asleep. He could sleep through
anything! An atomic bomb could go off on our front lawn, and he
would sleep right through it. How could he possibly hear it over all of
that loud snoring? The minute his head hits the pillow, he is out for the
count, then weird sounds like recordings of Sasquatch vocalizations
erupt from the man's throat.

I hid under the covers from the lightning flashes and peals of
thunder amidst my husband's cacophony, and prayed that God would
dispatch Saint Michael, Saint Raphael, Saint Gabriel, and our Guardian Angels to shield all four house corners, with the fifth angel on the
roof to fling off any fallen trees! A loud crash interrupted my thoughts,
catapulting me from a supine to a seated position.

I yelled, "[Deleted]! Good God save us!"

Photo: Angel suncatchers.

An angel suncatcher fell from our bedroom window. The noise was so loud it could have woke the dead, but it woke Tommy instead. *Close enough.*

We both sat upright in bed staring at the window in a stupor. *Maybe we should start crazy gluing these angels to the windows?*

Whenever an angel fell, we cleaned its suction cup and put moisture on it before sticking it back onto the window. We have even replaced the suction cups. After my accelerated heartbeat began to gradually slow down, I sensed this was another response to my prayer, and gave thanks to our holy warrior angelic friends for hearing and responding to it, although we wished it would have been a bit more subtle.

An Angel Feather for a Neighbor

ONE MORNING, I was trying to console our neighbor Jim, who was grieving over the recent death of his wife, Pat. He often stopped by for a few minutes to chat and to reminisce. It must have been consoling for him to talk about her. She was a dear, sweet woman who also had a belief in God's Holy Angels. A wooden sign in their living room window displayed a message: BELIEVE.

It was a pleasure to know his wife, although it was only for a brief time. Visits with her were always enjoyable, as we chatted, and I heard stories about her family and children.

Photo: White feather on our lawn.

She was an admirable, beautiful soul, a wonderful example of a loving mother, and a devoted servant of God in Charity. It was not hard to sense the intense pain and darkness of Jim's sadness and loneliness, and it was heartbreaking how much he missed her. I prayed God would send him some kind of comfort from his terrible grief.

A little voice, like a whisper entered my heart, telling me to "Look down." At our feet was a white feather. I picked it up and gave it to Jim, knowing in my heart that it was meant for him. *Did Pat want us to know she was at peace and happy in Heaven with God and His Holy Angels, that she no longer suffered and did not want Jim to grieve over her having to leave this life?*

We believed a message of love and hope was sent through God's Holy Angels for him to keep the faith, and to believe their separation would not be permanent, that they would be together again one day in Paradise. We both felt tranquil from the consoling presence surrounding us. After a few moments of silence, Jim decided to go back home. He told me he wanted to find a safe place to keep the feather.

I went inside my house, sat down, and read my daily prayers. Petitions were offered for his family to feel the peacefulness God allowed His Holy Angels to send the two of us a few minutes ago, which miraculously transpired on the front lawn.

One of our angel suncatchers fell from the dining room window onto the floor.

This was something we were getting used to.

I picked it up, then went over to Jim's house and rang his doorbell. When he opened the door, I held the angel suncatcher up for him to see, not knowing quite what to say. A minute or two passed, then I told him what happened.

Did God allow His Angels to send a second message, in response to my prayer for their family? Hopefully they would also feel God's love and comfort during the grieving period of their beloved one's death.

Angels at the Rainbow Bridge

IN A PREVIOUS story, I mentioned that Dr. Seuss, the last of our three beloved bearded dragons, had passed away. We missed him terribly. He was such a sweet and lovable companion, a description not many people would possibly imagine about a dragon or, to be more specific, a lizard.

Dr. Seuss became instantly attached to my husband the day we got him from a breeder at a reptile show. We laugh when we think about how this precious little one chose us instead of us choosing him. He walked right up to Tommy, climbed up his arm, and gave him a kiss. Our other two bearded dragons were more like a mama's boy and a mama's girl. Although they loved Tommy very much, they tended to be attached to me, as they preferred to cuddle, be pampered, and doted on. Dr. Seuss was affectionate but favored being independent. He was the daredevil, adventurer, and the never-tiring explorer, usually getting into trouble and having to be rescued from some perilous situation. One of the many comical things about Dr. Seuss (and there were many) was that he seemed to possess some aspects of Tommy's personality, such as having no fear and the no-guts-no-glory attitude. He was a real character.

People walking past our property in all likelihood must have thought we had a rambunctious child running amok inside our house, because we were constantly yelling, "Seuss! Where are you and what are you up to now?" When we would not see him or hear his nails clicking on the hardwood floor as he walked or ran, it was apparent he was up to something. Or he was helplessly stuck underneath the living room couch. Videos captured his spunk and mischievousness, which forever kept us entertained.

Photo: Rainbow.

He was so affectionate and endearing to everyone he met. Smart, too. When the garage door went up around 5 p.m., he knew Tommy was home from work, and would look toward the door, waiting for him to enter, knowing that soon he would be taking Seuss out of his tank for some exercise, play time, and affection, maybe even for a nice ride in the car, a walk, or just some quality outside time with us. He was a little angel who watched over us from his tank. Tommy and I could swear he knew when we were talking about him.

After Dr. Seuss passed away, an angel suncatcher fell to the floor, and we recalled that same suncatcher falling when Buddy, our black lab, was put to sleep. We were once again granted comfort that Dr. Seuss could be in heaven with Buddy.

The two of them were totally inseparable. They even took naps together during the day. In the beginning, when we brought Dr. Seuss home, he was very jealous of Buddy, who was Tommy's dog. He wanted all of the attention! But, as time went on, these two bonded like cement and became the best of friends.

Dr. Seuss even grieved over Buddy's death. He became depressed and did not eat for weeks.

We wondered why the same angel suncatcher fell? Were the Holy Angels informing us that Dr. Seuss was in heaven and, when he crossed the Rainbow Bridge, he was greeted by his best friend, who had been there awaiting his arrival?

We could picture Buddy, excitedly wagging his tail upon Dr. Seuss's appearance, then taking flight over the bridge to reunite with him. If these two were not together again, they definitely would not be in Heaven. They loved each other too much. Thanks be to God for sending these four-legged little furry and scaly angels who shower us with their unconditional love, during their journey here with us on earth. They bring so much joy, laughter, faith and healing in so many of our lives.

May our beloved Draco Dracaena, Dr. Seuss, Ulysses, Buddy, and Gin-Gin be frolicking together in God's presence. Until we meet again, one day at the Rainbow Bridge,

Rest in Peace.

Top photo (left to right) Starr Rae holding Ulysses, Santa holding Draco Dracaena and Tommy holding Dr. Seuss. Middle photo: Gin Gin Starr Rae's dog. Circa 1984. And Bottom photo: Buddy and Tommy 1995.

"One day, we will see our animals again in the eternity of Christ. Paradise is open to all of God's creatures." —Pope Francis.

Photos:(left to right top row) Dr. Seuss and Tommy. 2001. Ulysses with his little bear. 2009. Mom and Draco Dracaena.1998.

(Left to right second row) Dr. Seuss with his angel pillow. Buddy and Dr. Seuss. Monty, our favorite neighborhood feral cat. Below: Random photos of cute animal friends.

Bicycle Angels

Tommy and I went for a bike ride one evening. We started out wearing shorts, but a gut feeling advised me to change into capris instead. The Holy Angels knew it would not be a good idea for me to go biking in a pair of shorts.

After heeding the message, we began our journey and biked a few miles for a refreshing treat. Ice cream or frozen yogurt are wonderful incentives for me to go biking or to walk a few miles. After arriving and enjoying our treat, we started the ride back home on our usual route. The sugar kicked in and we were cruising at a good pace until I rode up a steep hill too slowly, changed my mind midway, and attempted to turn around.

The angle, too steep for the handlebars, caused me to fall on my right hip, elbow, and knee. "Learn how to ride a bike," they said. "It would be fun," they said.

Fortunately, the fall was not too bad. A skinned knee and scratched elbow took the direct hit, and my head did not hit the ground. I knew it could have been much worse. Material from the capris buffered the fall, protecting me from a direct skin-to-pavement impact.

"For he commands his angels with regard to you, to guard you wherever you go. With their hands they shall support you, lest you strike your foot against a stone." (Psalm 91:11–12) (NABRE).

How embarrassing it would have been if anyone witnessed seeing me in such a discombobulated state, except my husband. It must have been one hell of a Kodak moment. Thank God I can laugh at myself and the many mishaps that tend to take place in my life. There are no ifs, ands, or buts about a sense of humor being a saving grace.

Thanks to God and my Holy Guardian Angel for sparing me from becoming badly hurt or becoming a spectacle in that neighborhood.

These unexpected instances will never bring to a screeching halt the enkindled spirit of a born-and-bred Jersey girl. After dusting myself off and getting my act together, I hopped back up onto the seat of my bad-ass neon green and pink cruiser bike, then rode it back home like a boss.

Photo: Starr Rae on her bike.

The Angel Bracelet

M ARIE, A FORMER coworker, gave me a beautiful angel charm bracelet one year for Christmas. I was deeply touched to receive such a thoughtful gift and wore it proudly. A few weekends later, Tommy and I enjoyed a day of random local adventures. When we stopped for dinner at a restaurant, I sadly discovered that my bracelet had slipped off my wrist somewhere during the day. Heartbroken, I called the places we visited and left our phone number in case it was found. Unfortunately, someone probably would pick it up and keep it, because it was a very pretty piece of silver jewelry.

There was an inscription inside its box that read: "I bring you good news of great joy for all people." *For "all people?" Was the message meant for someone else besides me?* I called upon God's Holy Angels and Saint Anthony, known as the patron saint of lost items, as many miracles have been attributed to him. He earned the title when someone walked off with his book of psalms, which were immediately returned after the person saw a startling apparition of him. Yikes! I bet that person thought twice before doing something like that again!

We prayed that goodness would work through the bracelet, protecting it from destruction, and to send a positive message to whoever might find and possibly keep it. Hopefully, it would bring joy, lift their heart and soul, and provide healing if needed. It may not have been meant for me after all, which was okay. God's will be done. It was just a bummer such a gracious gift was lost. Three weeks passed. We assumed the bracelet was gone forever. However, miracles do happen!

A message was on our voice mail one night from a woman who was in the process of moving her business. She found a pretty silver charm bracelet in the parking lot of a shop we had visited. It had gotten mixed up inside some boxes and forgotten about until that afternoon, while she was sorting through supplies. The woman who owned the shop kept our phone number in a drawer and called us with the good news. Upon returning her call and giving a perfect description of the bracelet, she told me it was the bracelet I had been searching for and she would safely keep it in her possession until we were able to pick it up the following weekend.

Wow! What were the chances of getting my bracelet back after three weeks? It seemed like there was no chance at all. But we received a chance, an angel chance!

Even though it was found in an active parking lot, it was not damaged by any vehicles running over it, nor did the elements affect its condition. It was returned to us in nearly perfect shape and did not need much of a cleaning. We were confident someone or something was watching over it, another reminder we are in good company. Some things are meant to be, like getting back my nativity bracelet with the sparkling angel charms and the star of Bethlehem.

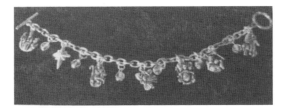

Photo: Nativity bracelet.

Angel in the Church Pew

S EVERAL YEARS AGO, after attending a women's weekend retreat, I went to church the following week and recognized a woman sitting in one of the pews, a few rows back from the front of the church, who was on the retreat. During mass, a strong feeling came over me, and a tiny whisper inside said, "Go up to her and say 'Hello' after mass." I thought, *You're kidding, right? I will feel awkward and stupid.*

I did not have the courage to be that outgoing, to approach someone I did not know, just to say "Hello." Then what? Alone in the pew, I sat there and argued with God, or whoever put what seemed like a crazy notion into my head.

Am I starting to go completely bonkers? The feeling insisted.

It had taken some time, but in the long run, I learned to trust these feelings, give in to them, and just go with it. Something good would generally come from it.

Photo: Our Beautiful Church.
Used with permission.

I managed to gather up some courage and walk up to the front of the church when the mass ended, slide into the pew next to her, turn and sheepishly say, "Hello, fellow retreatant." My face was probably red as a tomato, not knowing what to expect from this stranger.

What would she think? Who is this crazy redhead? What does she want?

Surprisingly, she remembered me from the retreat. We talked a short while, then went our separate ways. The following week I went back, and she was there again, leading a group to pray the rosary.

Despite not knowing how to pray it, I felt driven to join in with her and the others. At the conclusion, she reached into her purse and handed me a booklet on the devotion.

The following week, she placed into my hand a gift of rosary beads from a pilgrimage she made to Medjugorje, a town in Bosnia and Herzegovina, known for its apparitions of Mary, the Blessed Mother, which started in 1981 with six local children. The apparitions continue to this day.

The rosary is a meditation with repetitive prayers focused on the lives of Jesus and Mary. It is divided into four sets of mysteries: the Joyful Mysteries, the Sorrowful Mysteries, the Glorious Mysteries, and the Luminous Mysteries. Meditating on each mystery, we gain a better understanding of how to become more at peace and more Christ like. It became a powerful guiding force in my life.

My treasured friendship with Fely grew through the years. She became a trusted spiritual mentor who taught us a tremendous amount about our faith. We are positive we are not the only ones who have witnessed and have been inspired by her shining example of how a true and dedicated Christian should live their life. We feel blessed that God's Holy Angels brought us together.

Cemetery Angels

O N MY WAY to work one day, I drove over to the cemetery to visit my father's grave. After proceeding through the gate and continuing past the entrance, there was a small statue of an angel alongside the tombstones at the edge of the road. It looked strangely out of place, which, of course, sparked my curiosity.

Feeling drawn to it, I pulled the car over, then walked over to read the inscription on the small plaque beneath the statue. It held the dates 2005–2010, and was for a little boy who was only five years old. Deep sadness filled my heart for this little one, taken so early in life, and especially for his parents. How difficult and heartbreaking it must be to lose a child so young. The somber scene roused me of my own mortality. *God, what happened to this little boy, and why? What about all of these other people buried at this cemetery alongside him, who was taken so soon? Did they live their lives the best they could, to their potential, and serve you with a generous, merciful, and loving heart? Am I doing a good job of it myself?*

Compelled to leave a token of love for this little one, and a sign of faith and hope for his family, I reached into my pocket and pulled out one of my Saint Michael coins, placed it on the arm of the angel, then stood there staring at it for a moment. I trusted it would be received as a powerful message.

"He will wipe away every tear from their eyes, and there shall be no more death or mourning, wailing or pain, [for] the old order has passed away." (Revelation 21:4) (NABRE).

I said a prayer for the family he left behind, and for his little soul to rest in peace. Shortly after, I walked back to the car. It had been quite some time since I visited my father's grave, and the guilt of not making the time to go hit me. The worst part was that he was buried in a cemetery not far from my workplace. It seemed like there was never any time, as I was always in a rush, running late, or some other excuse. The reality of the moment struck like the bell on a clock. Time goes by way too quickly.

Despite my bad memory, something guided me straight to my father's tombstone. After driving past several rows of them, one appeared with an angel on it, and my eyes were drawn to the one directly behind it.

It was my dad's tombstone.

Thanks to God's Celestial GPS for guidance. I could not help but wonder if Dad was on the welcoming committee when that pure and innocent little one made his appearance at the Gates of Paradise.

Photo: (left) little boy's grave and (right) grave of Starr Rae's father.

Orchids and Angels

Hoping to get my mind off an ultrasound scheduled for later in the afternoon, I took a ride to the store to buy some light bulbs. A beautiful display of blue orchids was arranged on a table in the nursery section of the store. We never owned one because it would have been an expensive gamble, comparable to playing Russian roulette. Likely, the plant would end up dead and buried at the bottom of our trash can.

An employee working in the nursery maintaining the lovely flowers noticed my interest and struck up a conversation with me about

them. I mentioned how beautiful the plants were, but added that I could not bring myself to pay thirty dollars for a plant I knew nothing about, and that would probably be sentenced to death within a week. He instructed me on their proper care, then mentioned that one of the plants was marked down because it was accidentally knocked over and its pot broke. He offered it to me for two dollars, if I would be interested in getting one to try out.

It would need orchid food, a new pot, and more orchid potting mix to keep it happy. Everything came to just under ten dollars. It sure does pay to be in the right place at the right time. The Holy Angels made my day a whole lot brighter by placing a gorgeous plant in my shopping basket that morning.

Photo: Our beautiful orchid.

Upon my return home, it was repotted into a new, brightly colored pot, put into a sunny spot, offered a prayer for its survival, then given plenty of tender loving care. Several years passed and it seemed content as it grew strong, vibrant, and healthy. The photo below was taken eight years ago, the day when I forgot to buy light bulbs at the store.

As for my ultrasound, the technician told me it would take thirty minutes to complete. *Might as well do the rosary.* At the second Hail Mary, she declared, "You are done!" The test did not even take five minutes! Was this a positive sign?

On my way home, an accident occurred not far from where we live. A truck ran a red light and hit a SUV. If I had left the hospital sooner, I would have had a good chance of being involved in the accident. Thank God nobody got hurt.

I remembered asking God to send Saint Michael for protection that morning and also for Saint Raphael to journey in the car with me during the day. Their presence was felt upon my arrival home.

As for the ultrasound, it turned out fine.

Heavenly Patio Furniture

S PONTANEOUS ADVENTURES CAN be fun when you hop in the car and go without making any definite plans. Take a chance, trust God's Holy Angels, and permit them to be your GPS, which I personally call, "Going Places Special." If you give them permission to plan an escapade and your destination, you can count on something out of the ordinary to turn up. The only requirement is to just trust and believe they will come through for you.

Tommy often asks, "Where do you want to go? What do you want to do?"

I tell him, "Just get in the car and drive, God's Holy Angels will guide us!"

A little whisper tells us to turn left, or right, or take the next exit. We have learned to listen, and it has rewarded us with some incredible wonders.

Once, we saw this beautiful patio set at a garden center, located off a busy highway. We drove over for a closer look, and discovered it was a magnificent table and chair patio set made of concrete, beautifully designed in angel wings! How often do you come across something as charming and unique as that? We delighted in it, soaked up some sun, then left, hoping others would experience the same divine connection.

Photo: Tommy and Starr Rae enjoying some cool patio furniture.

A Warning Sent

T WO ANGEL MESSAGES arrived. Were they a heads up to provide strength for upcoming trials, or to expect something awesome to happen? At times, their messages can be hard to discern. Are the messages from God's Holy Angels or from the evil ones, hoping to cause distress? Are they mysterious, obvious, uplifting, or upsetting? Regardless, we should keep in mind that God is in charge, and either way He will take care of us. Examples of messages are usually items that have pictures of angels, or something that would easily relate to angels.

I received the first message during the day. It came by mail and was pleasant, an angel day planner. The following day, our next-door neighbor, Kelly, came over and gave me a little pocket shield of Saint Michael that she found in a store, and thought of buying it for me. *Was God preparing me for a future event by sending a message of strength through His Servant, Saint Michael?* A troubling phone call was received shortly after, from another doctor's office, telling me that three tests needed to be scheduled to find out if I had

Photo: Angel cloud formation in the sky.

Meniere's Disease. They requested it be done the following week, along with a brain MRI including contrast.

A trustworthy doctor had warned me many years ago not to allow nurses or technicians to attempt a blood draw, or to put IVs in my arms. The veins on my hands are surfaced and easier to access, so it is less painless, unlike the ones in my arms. The inside of the arms by the elbows are tender points for people who have been told they have Fibromyalgia, something a few doctors diagnosed me with after my battles with Lyme Disease.

Unfortunately, so far, I have found that many people in the medical field ignore my requests and insist upon poking several times at my arms first, as if I was their pincushion. Many have even gone to great lengths in constructing a narrative to convince me they are more skilled than anyone else and hold supremacy in their dominion. Despite their efforts to persuade me, all I hear is, "Wha, wha, blah." They sound like Charlie Brown's teacher.

It would be easier to nail gelatin to a tree than to get some of these people to listen.

What an ordeal! It is more stressful than the procedure itself! Doctors should prescribe a sedative to take an hour before arriving at the appointment.

Luckily, the following week, the MRI went fairly easily. The tech was notably compliant and put the contrast needle into my hand painlessly and without a fight. I sensed God and Saint Michael were there the entire time, holding my hand and comforting me during the imaging test.

The messages God allows His Holy Angels to send are to remind us of their presence in our lives, whether it is to share in our joys or to send us comfort and strength during difficult moments. These are blessings we should acknowledge and be thankful for.

God's Time Is Always Right

I N THE PRECEDING story, our neighbor Kelly, gave me a little Saint Michael pocket shield. Touched by her act of kindness, and wanting to give her something back, I mentioned that her father Jim was included in one of the angel stories chronicled in the book I was in the process of writing. A copy of the story was promised to her via email by the end of the day, however operating difficulties in the evening prevented me from sending it to her. Both Tommy and I made a few attempts to send the story to her, but it was futile.

Two weeks later, the promised story, which had almost been forgotten, popped into my mind. Our computer was still not cooperating, so I decided to hand write the story. I felt embarrassed over how long it had taken.

If we depended on the computer to do the work, Kelly, who is much younger than we are, would be living in a nursing home by the time she received it.

Unexpectedly, we received some beautiful angel cards in the mail that day. When the story was completed, I placed it inside one of the prettiest cards in the collection. It was brightly colored and very cheerful. A little whisper inside told me it was the perfect one to send.

Meanwhile, next door, Jim and Kelly's sister Kim were on their way out. Fortunately, I happened to look out the living room window and noticed they were getting into their car, so I hurried over to ask if Kelly was home. The desire to give her the story had become quite urgent. They said Kelly went to the emergency room the previous night, as she had been having excruciating pain. She was admitted into the hospital after the doctors ordered some tests and discovered a huge kidney stone, which needed immediate medical intervention.

I apologized for my tardiness in delivering the long overdue story, which I promised to her two weeks ago, and suggested both of them read the letter also. It was the story about the message we believed God delivered through His Holy Angels to Jim and I from his recently deceased wife, Pat. Originally titled "Angel Comforts for a Neighbor," the story went through several changes and currently has the title "An Angel Feather for a Neighbor." (See page 54 for the story.)

As they drove away to visit Kelly, that small, familiar whisper entered my heart again as I headed back home. But this time, it was not so small, it came out loud and clear. It said "God's time is always right!"

Angel comforts for a neighbor

One morning, in our front yard ,I tried consoling my neighbor who was grieving over his wive's recent death from cancer. There was solace reminiscing about her, a woman who also believed in angels.

A sign in their living room window said "BELIEVE."

It was a pleasure to know his wife, however, only for a brief time. Our visits were always enjoyable. We would chat, and I'd listen to stories about her family, and children. She was a sweet, beautiful woman, a loving mother and an amazing servant of God in Charity.

Photo: Part of the original title and story.

Larry the Homeless Angel

O N OUR WAY to a campground one year, Tommy and I stopped at a McDonald's for a quick lunch. Afterward, when we prepared to leave, we saw a man rummaging through a garbage can, asked if he was hungry, and offered to buy him something to eat. He eagerly responded, "Yes," so we went back inside with him and ordered him some food.

The three of us sat at a table and he shared his story with us. His name was Larry. Originally from Black River Falls, Wisconsin, he moved to California, lost his job, became down on his luck and homeless, so he decided to go to New York for temporary work. Hitchhiking his way there, he would eventually make his way to Maine, where family would help him.

He had the most indescribable blue eyes. Tommy, who has blue eyes, also noticed and commented on how bright his eyes were. Looking into them was like gazing into a cloudless, clear blue sky. Larry was polite and very well-mannered. We were under the impression he was happy just being in our company, and his only desire was to get from point A to point B. When asked where he was staying, he told us he had a sleeping bag under the highway bridge. Even though it was raining, it did not seem to concern him the least bit.

I felt compelled to find him a safe and dry place to stay overnight. While Tommy and Larry conversed, I excused myself and discreetly went across the street to a hotel to inquire about getting him a room for the night. There was an event downtown and there were no rooms available. Was there a local Salvation Army in the area? The manager looked up their phone number and found out the location was in the opposite direction of where we were headed, and too far to walk. Our car was jam packed with camping equipment, and I was not certain it would be safe for just one of us to drive a complete stranger in the opposite direction of where we were headed. Upon my return to the

McDonald's, Larry told us he was planning to go to the truck stop across the road. Later in the evening, he said he would try to hitch a ride from one of the truckers. He never asked us for a ride or money.

When we walked with him back outside into the parking lot, he turned toward us, smiled, and graciously thanked us for the food, money, and the company. Then he said "Goodbye." Seconds later, we turned to wave goodbye to him, but he had vanished! We drove around the building and parking lot to look for him, but he was nowhere to be seen.

A sign was above the truck stop: Loves, another word for Charity. As we pulled out of the McDonald's, I mentioned it to Tommy.

As we continued on the way to the campground, we learned that a terrible accident had occurred on the highway involving several cars and a tractor trailer. Traffic was backed up, bumper to bumper, for miles delaying us three hours from our destination. Tommy calculated the time, realizing we could have been involved in the accident had it not been for the interaction with Larry.

We felt grateful for meeting Larry and the opportunity to be charitable to him. But was Larry, in fact, the one who was actually being charitable? Was he one of God's Holy Earth Angels, sent to delay our travel, and possibly deliver us from a hazardous accident? We chuckled at the idea. It was, indeed, an unusual experience.

The traffic began to disperse, and the speed limit returned to normal. A tractor trailer passed us, and Tommy gasped. It was from Black River Falls, Wisconsin!

Chills ran down our spines.

As we traveled up the road, a billboard appeared with a beautiful angel on it, an advertisement for a forge. The magnificent image was imbedded in my mind the entire trip.

On our way home, we stopped at the forge to purchase an angel pin with the same design as the one on the billboard, along with an ornament of an angel looking down upon a sleeping person. Little did we know this ornament would also become a treasured purchase and a story would be written about it down the road.

Every year, the beautiful ornament hangs on our Christmas tree, a reminder of when we met Larry and were spared from possible disaster. We often think of him, and are sure he arrived safely to his destination, without needing to hitch a ride to get to it either.

Photo: The Archangel Raphael Leaving the Family of Tobias.
Rembrandt. 1637. Public Domain.

Do Angels Have Backups?

A MAN'S VOICE SPOKE to me in a dream one morning, saying he was sending me another angel, and asked if I would accept it with love in my heart. My impression was that it was God's voice. *Another angel?! Am I too much for one angel to handle? Did God decide to send my guardian angel a backup? Or did mine just need a break, and God was sending another to relieve it for a while, until mine could catch its breath?*

This was perplexing. Catholics are taught that everyone has only one guardian angel assigned to us at the moment of our conception. But, according to the Bible, there are many angels.

"I looked again and heard the voices of many angels who surrounded the throne and the living creatures and the elders. They were countless in number." (Revelation 5:11) (NABRE).

Photo: Advent ornament created by Wendell August Forge. Mercer, Pennsylvania. Used with permission.

Can more than one angel be assigned occasionally for times when we are being impetuous or are in danger? Are all those extra set of wings floating around Heaven on call, waiting for God to send them on special missions? Does God send them to earth temporarily for extreme emergency situations? Still baffled, I prayed for an answer. If it was God in my dream and it was His will to send another angel to temporarily give mine a hand, so be it! Not my will be done, but His! I hope the answers to these million-dollar questions will be answered one day. Perhaps God has a secretary up there, printing out Q and A sheets for all of us who are still down here waiting for answers.

What if God was truly planning to send another angel down to help out my guardian angel? Should it be given a name? Not a good idea. In the past, I admit to doing this unknowingly for my guardian angel, then regretting it after finding out it is not our birthright to name God's angels. Is it not exclusively God's entitlement to name His own purest creation? Doesn't it make sense that it would be safest for us to call upon them as Holy Warrior Angels of Almighty God or of Jesus Christ? The demons will not be able to respond and deceive us into thinking they are the good angels we have named and called upon whom we trust.

We should also never worship angels, for only God is worthy of worship. It is even confirmed by angels in the Bible not to worship them, as they, like us, are God's creation.

"I fell at his feet to worship him. But he said to me, 'Don't! I am a fellow servant of yours and of your brothers who bear witness to Jesus. Worship God.'" (Revelation 19:10) (NABRE)

In the previous story, after a camping trip we stopped at a forge on our way home and purchased an angel pin and a Christmas ornament of an angel smiling down upon a sleeping person, it was titled "Angel in a Dream." A connection was made, as we put the ornament on our Christmas tree, of our encounter with, "Larry the Homeless Angel," and the possibility of God sending my guardian angel, a backup.

My Saint Michael Poster for the Women's Retreat

M Y FRIEND CATHY, from our parish, invited me to join the women's retreat team a few years ago. I was still in the midst of battling some post-Lyme disease symptoms and was not sure if I could dedicate myself to this huge commitment. So, initially the invitation was turned down. Tommy and I were at church one day and saw Cathy, sitting a few pews in front of us with the women who would be on the team. Chris, another one of my friends, joined the team and was sitting there with them.

Again, came that small persistent whisper in my heart, "Do not be afraid. Trust God. Go for it. Join the retreat team!" I thought, *Oh brother, here we go again!*

Eventually giving in, I turned to whisper in Tommy's ear, "I'm going to sit with the women in front of us." My poor husband probably wondered why his wife did not want to sit in church next to him. Winking, I said I would explain later.

A surprised look came over Cathy's face when I made my appearance and motioned for her to move over so I could sit next to her. Trusting God's Holy Angels to make this work, I announced I was joining the retreat team. The next couple of weeks, our team prepared for the retreat, named ADORO, under the patronage of Our Lady of the Blessed Sacrament. We were asked to give a report and design a poster on one of our favorite saints. Guess who I chose?

My artwork was proudly displayed to a friend before the retreat. She pointed out how I got a bit "Carried away" when I used brightly colored feathers for wings. Saint Michael looked more like a peacock or a Thanksgiving centerpiece than one of God's Holiest Angels. *What in the world was I thinking?*

The retreat turned out to be both rewarding and successful. After spending some prayer time, our team did two comical skits for the retreatants. My friend Donna and I kneaded dough and ended up in a flour fray during a presentation of "Baking bread the 2,000-year-old Roman way." In the second skit, I impersonated my favorite actress/comedian and dressed up with Carmela, another fun teammate. We wore silly wigs, then proceeded to stomp on some plastic grapes. Shortly after, we feigned a hilarious battle in the grape vat. Everyone roared with laughter. Donna, Carmela, and I had a hard time keeping our faces straight, but I think we pulled it off pretty well. What a fantastic memory! I'm glad I listened to that inner voice.

Photo: Starr Rae's Saint Michael poster, before and after shots.

ADORO Angels

W HEN SOMETHING GOOD or bad is about to happen, as you now know, our angel suncatchers become involved. One day, one fell from our bedroom window, a common occurrence in our home. We think it is God's Holy Angels' way of saying, "Heads up, be on the lookout, and do not lose faith."

A rash reappeared on my foot, which had started a few weeks prior. Luckily, we had cortisone and I applied some right away. The pharmacist thought it was a touch of poison ivy and, after a few days of application, it seemed to be gone. I stuck the suncatcher back up onto the window, then went about my business. Two days later, it fell again. *Now what?* The rash was back. It was bright red, horribly itchy, and spreading to both legs. *Was it from a tick bite?* We were not in any risky areas. After having Lyme disease twice, it became a regiment to be vigilant and constantly check ourselves in grassy areas, or anywhere ticks could possibly be hiding. A can of OFF became a permanent fixture in the garage and in the back seats of our cars.

The cortisone was applied to the rash, then off to bed we went, hoping it would soothe the itch, but it got worse. Now, it was over my entire body, along with a terrible burning sensation, and my face looked sunburned. Desperately, I jumped into the shower, praying God would send relief. As water sprayed on me, the small familiar voice inside shouted, "Enzymes!" God's Holy Angels were warning me about the new digestive enzyme we had

Photo: (Top left) Statue of The Blessed Mother. (Right) ADORO card designed by Carmela S. Both used with permission.

started taking when the rash first appeared. Apparently, a dermatological reaction was coming through my pores, causing the itching and burning. After changing my pajamas, the sheets and pillowcase, then dragging myself back into bed, we prayed for the terrible burning to ease up.

Tommy was on the brink of driving me to the Emergency Room. I closed my eyes and struggled through a decade of the rosary. A magnificent vision came into my mind of a beautiful lady who was comforting me in her arms. The affliction eased, leaving me with a feeling of peacefulness and a sense of security and trust knowing that God had heard my cries. He sent His Holy Angels to rescue me.

The next morning, my mom called to share something interesting that happened in the middle of the night. She was awakened by a voice that came into her head, that she thought said, "Dora." It corrected her and said, "No, I said ADORO."

Mom was clueless to what this meant, and I was speechless. She did not know about the rash or the name of the women's retreat I had been on that year. After a moment of silence, I told her what ADORO was, and about the awful rash that went away and returned, then about my vision of a beautiful lady who held and comforted me. My mother was stunned. *Was our Blessed Mother, The Queen of all Angels, the one who came to soothe me in my distress the previous night, then she informed my earthly mother about it?*

Rooftop Angels

T OMMY AND I needed a time out, so we planned an unusual evening getaway from a stressful situation. We checked into a hotel, then picked up takeout for dinner. This was not something we planned to do. We sent prayers for God to intercede for us. Soon after, we noticed a multitude of birds perched on the tiles of the roof outside our hotel room window.

Wow, what's with all these birds? Then we recalled seeing the beautiful angel sign which greeted us at the hotel entrance. The next morning, we heard several people singing in the hallway. It was uplifting and reminded us to pray over the difficult situation awaiting us. People make mistakes. Were we being too sensitive and just needed to move forward in a positive direction? After deciding to check out of our room earlier than we had planned, we approached our car in the parking lot. There was something huge and white on it.

"Arrgghh, those bleep! birds pooped all over our windshield!"

I recalled once hearing it was a sign of good luck when birds drop a bomb on your car. If it was true, we were being sent off with a hearty number of blessings!! After a good scrubbing, we drove away light-hearted, with an optimistic attitude.

Photo: A little bird about to drop a bomb?

Messages on Facebook

S OMETIMES FRIENDS AND family who are on social media, whether Facebook or other sites, have the potential to ease our minds from our trials and tribulations. They can lift our spirits when their inspiring posts speak directly to our hearts. These marvelous posts usually spring from our closest friends, family, and, surprisingly at times, even from total strangers.

Perky messages can perform wonders when we are in the midst of life's daily struggles and are not able to be near our loved ones physically. It is a wonderful way to stay connected and to reconnect with

Photo: Mom and Dad's garden angel.

healthy relationships from the present and the past. Good examples include family, high school friends, and coworkers. Many times, when things get to be too much to deal with, going online and taking a break from it all can be like taking a dose of sweet-tasting medicine.

On my Facebook feed, there is always someone who can be counted on for humorously speaking their mind or posting an inspirational or funny article. A post once stated something like, "No matter how crummy the day can get, do not forget about the holy angels who are looking out for you, even if you cannot see them." It was a post that could have been sent from God's Holy Angels or from Saint Michael the Archangel himself. The Holy Angels tend to be very creative in finding ways to get our attention and inform us that everything will be alright, to stop worrying, and to remember

God is in control! Most of the time, this is easier said than done, but it is something we must keep striving to do!

I am certain that in my life, there have been many times their heavenly messages have gone straight over my head and been unintentionally overlooked. It is important to make an effort to have an open mind, stay alert, and pay close attention to what is happening around us in our differing environments. We must set our sights in order to be more in tune to their messages. In time, with practice, it will teach us how to enhance the awareness of their guiding presence in our lives. Only then will we gain the ability to acknowledge and thank them for their directives. We will become fully alert that the miraculous messages they send are blessings from God.

A Message from Heaven

OUR FRIEND JUNE posted a photo of her husband, Pedro's, tombstone on Facebook on what would have been his sixtieth birthday. A deep sadness entered my heart, imagining the sorrow she must have felt. Pedro was such a sweet and incredible man who unfortunately suffered a long time from Gulf War Syndrome and pulmonary obstruction before passing away. June took such loving care of him, despite having a disability herself. She walked with a cane or used a motorized cart to get around, but we never heard her complain. She was always so upbeat and positive.

June and Pedro were so devoted and in love with each other. They were an inspiration to many, especially to Tommy and I. A fantastic memory of them came to mind when Tommy and I were talked into attending a medieval camping event called "Pennsic War" by a few friends. The event took place at a campground in Butler County, Pennsylvania. More than 500 acres were annually transformed into a medieval town, hosting an attendance of more than 10,000 people dressed in period clothing. Excitement filled the air as royals, gentry, merchants, and peasants took part in classes teaching fine arts and martial activity from the period. This lasted for two fantastic weeks.

Tommy and I fenced in the Rapier Field Battle the second year we attended, and our side won! There were hundreds of fencers against us, so we did not last long in the skirmish, but it was a lot of fun to be involved in.

June and Pedro camped next to us in their lovely pavilion tent. We joked over how easy it would be to find us in this medieval environment. Our orange polyester non-period (mundane) tent stuck out like a sore thumb. You could tell beyond the shadow of a doubt that we were newbies.

We were pre-registered in the disability area due to my Lyme Disease the first year we attended, and our tent was assigned near a portable toilet, or, as medievalists would profess, The Privy. Never in our lives had we seen portable toilets kept so clean as the ones were there. A middle-eastern coffeehouse was directly across from our campsite and was open until 3 or 4 a.m. The privy door slammed all night long, which kept us awake. For this reason alone, we were not exactly happy campers. However, we loved being at Pennsic.

Pedro spent most of his time in bed on an oxygen machine, or occasionally he sat in a chair. We shared some of our spiritual experiences with each other. I even told him about my near-death experience. One afternoon, we went to get him ice cream and June came along with her electric scooter. Upon our return, the four of us relaxed at their campsite and enjoyed the special treats. It was a day filled with many blessings, one that we would always hold dear in our hearts and memories.

When Pedro passed away, June embroidered beautiful favors, which we proudly wore on our rapier belts at every event, in tribute to him, especially when we competed in fencing tournaments. We felt honored and blessed to have been in his presence, although just for a short time, and felt privileged to call him friend.

Presently, as I prepared dinner, my heart spoke to him, "We miss you so much, I wish there was a way you could let us know you are happy and at peace." I offered prayers for him and for June to find consolation in easing the sorrow this day must have brought her.

Two solar lights in front of our house suddenly turned on, lighting up our statue of Saint Michael, which had not been lit for a few weeks. The lights were so bright that they were visible from the back of our house.

The last time we saw our Saint Michael statue lit was late fall, before the snow had started. The lights had become so dim that we planned on going to the store during the week to replace them.

It was amazing how bright our front porch suddenly became, especially because there was not much sunshine during the week. We doubted there was even enough light to recharge the batteries.

Dinner was put on hold as I dashed over to the computer to send an email to June, expressing our condolences, and the sadness we felt seeing the photo of Pedro's tombstone. I told her my heart spoke to him and how I wished for a message that he was happy and at peace. It was hard to contain myself while telling her about the solar lights that all came on at once, illuminating our Saint Michael statue, after not being lit for weeks. It happened so abruptly, as if Pedro knew how sorrowful June was and had heard the loving thoughts sent his way.

Did our merciful God allow Pedro to send a message, to ease the pain June must have been enduring that day? Tommy and I believe it was sent by God's Holy Angels to send her comfort until the day when they will be reunited again.

Photo: Our orange, extremely non-period tent next to June and Pedro's. Used with permission. Story of Pennsic. Used with permission.

Footsteps on a beach

I SLEPT ON AND off most of the day due to the flu and a stomach virus. After finally dozing off, I dreamed of walking on a beach. The sun, brightly shining, made everything around me feel extremely hot, as it beat down on me. It was difficult to walk in the sand, and exhaustion was starting to set in. Suddenly, I felt myself being lifted up and carried by two very strong arms.

Much to my surprise, it was Jesus carrying me back to where my walk had originally started. There was also a presence walking alongside of us, which was not seen or heard, until Jesus laid me down upon a blanket. We both turned to look toward the presence, then heard its voice begin to say, "They call me..."

I awoke at that moment and did not hear the rest of the name. Could this presence have been my Guardian Angel? Whenever an angel appeared to someone in the Bible, its name was unknown, with the exception of Saints Michael, Gabriel, and Raphael, whose names are in the Bible.

"At that time there shall arise Michael, the great prince, guardian of your people." (Daniel 12:1) "'I am Gabriel, who stand before God. I was sent to speak to you and to announce to you this good news.'" (Luke 1:19) "I am Raphael, one of the seven angels who stand and serve before the Glory of the Lord." (Tobit 12:15) (NABRE).

Why did the dream cut off the moment the presence was about to identify him or herself? Was it because God did not want me to know what its name was?

"What is your name, that we may honor you when your words come true? The angel of the Lord answered him, 'Why do you ask my name? It is wondrous." (Judges 13:18) (NABRE).

Was God confirming the ability to give names, or to know the names of our guardian angels He created, was in His authority only?

This is something to think about. Who are we to know the name of, or to name, a holy creature God himself has created? Perhaps God has already given them names and only he knows what they are. Unless we are very pure and holy people whom He has chosen and granted special permission to, I doubt this would happen, because the Holy Angels serving God are pure themselves.

Before falling asleep, I had a fever that broke during the dream. It was replaced with a feeling of refreshment, new energy, and hunger.

Pondering over the beautiful, heavenly dream of Jesus rescuing me, along with the new friend walking alongside us on the beach, I offered prayers that this friend would continue to walk with us, not only in my dreams but also in my life, on this spiritual journey.

Photo: On the beach

Saint Michael's Approval

Tommy and I decided to do something fun over the weekend, then have dinner at one of our favorite vegetarian cafes. After being seated, a party of four came in and were told they had to wait for a table. We were seated at a table between two tables for two and told the waitress we would be willing to move over for the group so they could sit together and not have to wait.

The group was very appreciative as we scooted over to the next table to accommodate them. Shortly afterward, our waitress walked back over to our table and offered us a free dessert for volunteering to move over and make room for the group. We thanked her for the offer but graciously refused it, explaining it was unnecessary. There was no need to reward us. We were only being considerate toward others and doing the right thing.

She told us that some people who come into the cafe would not have been as compliant, even after she politely asked them to move over. I told her in a joking manner, "If it happens again, tell them the boss said to get up and move your lazy butts, you selfish and self-centered people!" The three of us laughed. It felt good to send some humor her way. She was a young, very sweet, hard–working, and proficient server.

A few seconds later, while we were waiting for our lunch to be served, a message appeared on my cell phone from a friend on Facebook. She randomly sent a beautiful photo of Saint Michael. I showed the photo to Tommy and said, "Wow! How interesting? Is Saint Michael sending a message to let us know he approves of what we did by moving over for that group? Maybe he is also agreeing with what I said to our waitress about the selfish, self-centered people who refuse to accommodate others? Perhaps his thoughts are in unison with mine, that they should get up and move their lazy butts?"

We both laughed. The photo could not have arrived at a more perfect moment.

"The thrones of the arrogant God overturns and establishes the lowly in their stead. The roots of the proud God plucks up, to plant the humble in their place. He breaks down their stem to the level of the ground, then digs their roots from the earth." (Sirach 10:14–16) (NAB).

Photo: Saint Michael Weighing Souls. Juan de la Abadia, 'The Elder.' 1470-1490. Public Domain.

Message on a Sidewalk

I N THE MIDST of a daily walk, my mind drifted. It seemed like God's Holy Angels had been out of touch with us for quite some time. A sorrowful feeling settled deep within my soul. *Who is it that has been out of touch? Perhaps it is not them, but us?* How true, we get so caught up in our lives or from distractions that we forget they are around us all the time, watching over us. We even forget to make time to pray. They could whack us over the head with a two-by-four and we would still miss the visible and obvious messages they are sending.

It occurred to me how important these walks had become. They were a motive for going outside, getting back in shape, connecting with nature, and providing a peaceful break from all the day's responsibilities.

I crossed the street, stepped up onto the sidewalk, and reflected on how we had grown to appreciate and love having the presence of God's Holy Angels in our lives. Something came into view on the sidewalk, *Holy cow! Are my eyes playing tricks on me?*

Photo: Message on a sidewalk.

There, on the sidewalk, written in dirt was a greeting. It said, "Hi!"

Completely dumbfounded, I wondered if it was another message from God's Holy Angels. It seemed pretty evident. Were they letting me know that no matter how far our thoughts can be from God or His Holy Angels, they are always hanging around and will never leave us, not even for one second?

An Angelic Eternity Scarf

O
NE COLD AND rainy afternoon, feeling discouraged and depressed over some of life's unpleasant circumstances and the drudgery of the day, I sat at the dining room table and began to cry. This does not happen often. I tend to be pretty positive and upbeat the majority of the time.

However, a friend posted an eye-opening email about all the trials we go through in life, especially as we get older. It mentioned the bad shape our country was in, with the cost of living and high gas prices, while there were not many jobs. It also discussed how corrupted, divided, and lost we have become, taking God out of schools, the government, and even Christmas. As sad as the situation was, I was sure there were more of us who wanted God back than not. The sound of the pouring rain and the post resonated in my heart. A mixed bag of emotions came to the surface, including the many sorrows of the world, some related to my own life, and questions not yet answered. It was the beginning of May, Lyme Disease awareness month. The previous day we tied a green ribbon to our mailbox, hoping that someday a cure would be found for all incurable diseases.

There was a package inside our mailbox when I went outside to fetch the mail.

Much to my surprise, upon opening it, was a beautifully knitted scarf made by Daria and Melissa, two of our dear friends. Attached to it was a lovely card: "Here is an eternity scarf, consider it a hug, put it on when you need some love, and then think of us." The unexpected gift arriving on that particular day was emotionally moving. Even though the day started out cold, rainy, overall crummy, and it brought me down a bit, the realization of how blessed I am to have such thoughtful and caring friends lifted my spirit tremendously.

They sent a breath of fresh air my way. The thought of them spending so much of their free time to create this special gift, when they could have been doing something else, brought tears to my eyes. The timing was perfect, as usual. It was delivered on one of the crappiest and most depressing days, when it was most needed.

This very warm, pretty, and cherished gift has been worn on several special occasions, and the abundance of compliments keep coming. Since the day it was delivered into our mailbox, it has always been, and will always be, a reminder that my Earth Angel friends never fall short in their loving ability to send hugs my way, even when their hugs must travel from quite a distance away. I am blessed that many of them are in my life.

Photo: A beautiful knitted scarf.

Heart-Shaped Boxes and Angel Feathers

A COUPLE OF YEARS ago, a friend gave me a red, heart-shaped Valentine's Day box filled with an assortment of pretty multicolored bird feathers. She believed the angels came in the form of birds and had collected these feathers for quite a long time. There must have been at least 100 feathers inside the box, and the variations of beautifully colored feathers made me wonder what angels actually look like. *Do they really have feathers? If so, would they be different colors, sparkling white, or just clear?*

Because spirits are invisible to the human eye, not many can say for sure. Very few people have witnessed an angel's visual presence. The only accounts we are truly aware of are when they appeared to people in the Bible or to some of the saints. Those angels seemed to be formidable in appearance, unlike the pictures, paintings, or figurines we see, usually depicting them with imaginative human perceptions.

"The angel of the Lord appeared to them, and the glory of the Lord shone around them, and they were struck with great fear. The angel said to them, 'Do not be afraid, for behold, I proclaim to you good news of great joy that will be for all the people.' (Luke 2:9–10) (NABRE).

Photo: Heart-shaped box filled with feathers.

However, these messengers of God are known to appear in any kind of human form as God wills it, in a variety of sizes, shapes, and colors. Experiences with complete strangers, or Earth Angels, who show up out of nowhere when help is needed, can confirm this. It has happened many times to me while shopping in supermarkets or department stores. A person suddenly appears when something is on a shelf too high to reach or when an item cannot be found. They are either tall enough to reach what is needed, able to go get or find the item, or direct you to exactly what it is you are looking for. Once a lady appeared behind me, suggesting a different brand of gluten-free bread than the one I was in the process of searching for in the freezer. It turned out to be a much superior choice!

These Earth Angels can be short, tall, black, white, thin, fat, and from any walk of life, gender, nationality, and so on.

The friend who gave me the box of feathers struggled with a lot of hardships and many health issues. I sent prayers to the Holy Warrior Angels to guide her, and to direct peace into her heart. *Please God, send her as many blessings as there are feathers inside this heart-shaped box.*

The feathers were initially used on my poster of Saint Michael for the women's retreat in a previous story, but were changed to white instead.

My Husband's Work Van

I T WAS AROUND 3:00 a.m. Again, sleep was not on God's agenda for me. Tommy sensed my restlessness and reached over to hold my hand. Sleep comes easily for him, so he quickly drifted back off. Whenever sleep does not come, I add in additional prayers, asking God and His Holy Angels to protect my family, friends, and my husband as he's driving to or from work, while on his job, and so on.

The following day, Tommy called from his cell phone to tell me he could have been involved in a serious accident. His work van had suddenly become inoperable while he was driving. Engine power was lost, but he was still able to maneuver the van without colliding with the other vehicles on the highway and safely get off at the next exit. Thank God for his ability and skill to avoid getting into an accident, which could have harmed or killed not only himself but other drivers as well.

When he brought the van into the service station, the mechanics checked to see what was wrong with it, and he was told the van was working fine, there was nothing wrong with it. There was no explanation what caused the malfunction. It was a freak incident.

We were thankful God sent His Holy Angels to take over the wheel of the van and assist Tommy in avoiding a potentially dangerous situation. This may explain my restlessness from the night before. I must have had a premonition, which prevented me from being able to fall asleep. At the time, it could very well have been the cause of what prompted those additional prayers.

Photo: The Guardian Angel. Marcantonio Franceschini. 1716. Public Domain.

"Never travel faster than your Guardian Angel can fly!"
—Attributed to Mother Teresa.

An Angel Kiss During the Night

I OFTEN AWAKE AT 3:00 a.m. Catholics believe that 3:00 p.m is The Hour of Divine Mercy, when Jesus died on the cross to save us from our sins. Although Church tradition does not mention the time of 3 a.m, it's been believed to be the "devil's hour," when Satan mocks God during the opposite hour by manifesting large amounts of sin and demonic activity. Also, it is good to note that the absence of prayer from the Liturgy of the Hours is from 1 a.m. until dawn).

Sometimes, a person's name will just pop into my mind, with a strong urge to pray for them. If it is unknown who required the invocation, I ask God to send His Holy Angels to help the soul in need. This is the only rationalization of why I keep waking up suddenly at this same exact time. God knows His prayer warriors will make the connection and answer his call for prayer when needed.

Photo: Statue of angel with reflection in window.

One particular night it happened and, after my prayers were completed, a kiss from out of the darkness suddenly landed upon my lips. Instinctively, I turned to look where it came from. There was Tommy with a blissful look on his face. He suddenly awakened and something triggered him to give me a kiss! When questioned why he kissed me, he said it was because he thought I was asleep.

Because I was asleep?

The puzzled expression on his face revealed something deeper. Did angels rouse him from sleep, then whisper in his ear to give me a kiss? Perhaps it was another one of their creative ways to respond to our prayer requests?

Angels at the Wheel

I T WAS A Friday evening around 8:30 p.m. I had just finished a very busy day at work and decided to grab something quick to eat before starting the long drive back home. Thank God for the McDonald's approximately two or three miles up the road, which many a night was the source of my salvation. It relieved my hunger pangs and provided newfound energy to continue the trip homeward. A quick pick me up at the drive thru window normally generated enough stamina to get me home safe and sound.

This particular evening, after placing my usual order and proceeding to the pickup window, I heard the sound of glass crunching under one of my tires. A feeling of uneasiness swept upon me. *Oh my God! I think I drove over a glass bottle!*

After alerting the worker behind the pickup window about my current calamity, he handed over my bag of food, then sent someone out to sweep up the mess from under my tire. The idea of driving over a glass bottle, then having to drive 70 miles alarmed me a great deal. Nonetheless, after getting out of the car and doing a thorough investigation with the employee, all four tires were intact. I pulled into a nearby parking spot, opened my bag, and enjoyed my dinner. Then, back on the road that took me home.

While merging onto the highway, a lighted image resembling an angel with its wing's spread open appeared on the car's panel. I called Tommy from my cell phone.

"What the heck is this?"

He had no idea what it was or what it meant. I steered the car into the right lane and drove at a slower speed, in case it was a warning from God's Holy Angels. *Oh God, please get me home in one piece!* These signs happened so often that I immediately understood it to be either a message of comfort or a warning to be vigilant for upcoming danger or difficulties. My worst fear was that while driving one of my tires would blow out, leading to a loss of control over the car that would cause a serious accident. Attempting to stay calm and not allow anxiety to take over, I took a couple of deep breaths and tried to relax my muscles. *God, I trust you will get me home safe and sound.*

Most of the trip was spent in the right lane, crawling along the shoulder. It must have looked like I just got my driver's license or needed to turn it in. I offered prayers for my safety and for the other drivers for the next several miles. Within a short distance, a huge sign appeared on the side of the road, an advertisement: "My Three Angels."

God's Holy Angels were letting me know that I was heard, they had me covered! A relaxed feeling instantly came over me. Stepping on the gas pedal, I zipped back into the fast lane. What a relief it was from driving in the slow lane. It was not fun getting funny looks or the middle finger from the other drivers who were impatient with my snail-like driving.

The rest of the trip would be safe, smooth, peaceful, and pleasant, as I resumed driving at the normal speed. After pulling the car into our garage, Tommy checked the lighted image, which still remained on the car's panel. It indicated that one of the tires was either flat or needed air. We looked at each other in disbelief. *How in the world would I have been able to drive seventy miles without knowing one of the tires was flat? Ok, so maybe one needed air?*

None were flat or needed air. All four tires looked perfectly fine. We checked the tires three times and there was absolutely nothing wrong with them.

The next morning, we went into the garage, planning to go to the store, and were quite shocked to find one of the tires flat, and there was a chunk of glass in it! You have got to be kidding! *Why didn't we see the glass in the tire the night before?* The garage light was on when we checked all four tires thoroughly, and there was nothing there!

Did God's Angels intercede and protect me while driving home the previous night? Was our car securely bound upon the wings of Saint Michael, Saint Gabriel, and Saint Raphael. I recalled the huge sign that I saw on the side of the road on my way home that said My three angels. I was convinced.

Photo: The Three Archangels with Tobias. By Francesco Botticini.1467. Public Domain.)

Lost and Found

T HE HOUSE KEY was not on our key ring, and my Saint Michael medallion necklace was missing. This was very distressing. It was upsetting enough not being able to find my necklace, but we were a lot more concerned about the missing key. *What if someone found the key? They could get inside our house!* At the time, we did not have a house alarm. The thought of someone intruding inside our home was enough to scare me out of all my senses. We live in a safe neighborhood, but you never know. We do need to be more careful these days.

I thought about the key. *We went out last night. Could it be somewhere in the car?* We had already checked the car the previous night several times, but the tiny whispering voice told me to go and search for it again. Praying it might somehow appear, we opened the car door and searched the front, the back seats, and then the floor. Nowhere.

Photo: Angel tealight holder
with jewelry.

"Push the seat back, check again," said the little voice. Voila! There it was! Then, "Go into the bedroom and search for the necklace again." My heart began to race. Even though we already searched several times extensively, we went back to take a look one more time and, as God is my witness, there it was on the angel statue, where it is hung every night! Both of us checked the statue a few times previously, and it was not there, yet now it was!

I asked Tommy if he was playing tricks on me. He stopped, turned, and looked at me, then very seriously said "No." I knew he was not lying. We looked at each other and scratched our heads in amazement. No one else was in our house and, in case you are wondering, we both have good eyesight according to our ophthalmologist. *So, what in the world is going on? Do God's Holy Angels come to aid us when the evil ones take delight in causing us distress?* The demons are probably howling with laughter as they watch us run amok, desperately searching for our missing items. Could it be that the Holy Angels often come to bring us relief by returning items back to where they belong?

Cat-Man Bob

OUR DEAR FRIEND, who we lovingly referred to as "Cat-man Bob," lived up the street from us. He was a compassionate gentleman with a heart of gold who took care of several feral cats in our neighborhood. He befriended and fed the cats, and assisted us, along with some other neighbors, in the local Trap, Neuter, and Release Program, which manages free-roaming cat populations in a humane, structured manner. This man generously opened up his house and sunroom to the cats, usually in the winter, so they had a warm and safe place to stay, especially during bad snowstorms, and even provided a heater for them.

He loved cats very much, particularly his house cat named Princess Diana, a huge, domestic, orange-colored tabby that lived to be sixteen years old. His heart broke the day she passed away unexpectedly. We think God must have sent him these other feline friends for companionship, and to comfort him during his grief over her death.

One early afternoon, Cat-man Bob fell from his bed, and called us from his cell phone for help. Tommy and I rushed over to his house and waited with another neighbor for an ambulance to arrive, which transported him to the nearest hospital. The emergency medical technicians were not 100 percent sure, but they thought he had a stroke.

The next day, Tommy received a very strong feeling that we should go to visit Cat-man Bob in the hospital. Upon our arrival at his hospital room, we could tell he was experiencing a lot of pain, so we asked if he would like for us to pray over him. He eagerly accepted, so we stood on each side of his bed and prayed over him, and the pain finally started to ease.

He told us the prayers worked and he seemed more coherent and responsive to our presence. When one of the nurses came to check up on him, we asked what was wrong with our friend, and were told he had a very severe infection that required treatment, and he would have to be hospitalized for a few weeks. It came as a shock to Tommy and I, as before this incident he appeared to be healthy. We stayed by his bedside a while, then left to go home. A few days later, when things settled down, we planned to go back and visit him again.

Before we left his side, he asked us to take care of his cats. He loved them so much and was very concerned over their well-being. I promised that we would.

Early the following morning, the ringing of my cell phone woke me from a bad dream. A bit dazed and somewhat out of it, I reached over to answer the call to discover it was Cat-man's brother, calling to inform us that Cat-man had suddenly passed away during the night.

God's Holy Angels motivated Tommy to lead us on an important mission to visit our friend in the hospital and pray over him, unaware it would be the last time we would see him alive. Through divine intervention, and by the grace of God, we were commissioned to go forth with the ability to be instrumental in bringing our friend the prayers and comfort he needed. He died at peace, knowing his friends were there for him and would take care of his beloved cats.

We sought out a few kind and compassionate neighbors who would take good care of them.

Unfortunately, Tommy and I are allergic to cats, so we could not take any of them in. These Earth Angels took over feeding and watching over them. Some even adopted the cats and brought them into their homes after gaining their trust.

It was such a sad sight to see those poor cats wander around Cat-man's house shortly after he passed away. They looked lost and forlorn. Most likely, they wondered what had happened to their friend. Perhaps they thought he abandoned them, just like their former families had done, and grieved terribly over the loss of what was probably the first person who ever showed them love and compassion.

A few of his cats are still around and have been accepted by most of the neighbors, who feel compassion for them. They are aware that these unfortunate creatures were originally forsaken by their inhumane and heartless humans, and that it was not the cats' choice to be cast off.

It gives us consolation to conclude that Cat-man is in heaven, resting at peace, possibly basking in the sun next to his most beloved Princess Diana, knowing in his heart that a promise was kept.

Photo: Monty, Cat-man Bob's favorite feral cat.

If You Listen, You Can Hear the Angels Sing

MY CHIROPRACTOR ORDERED an X-ray of my back, which revealed a herniated disc in my neck and stenosis of my lower spine. He highly suggested that I order and commit to using a traction device twice a day, while lying in a horizontal position on the floor. I thought, *Oh, joy*.

Medical bills from the past several years had added up, from appointments with doctors, blood tests, procedures, and way too many prescriptions. This was just another thingamajig, with a hefty price tag attached. It would be used for a short while, then would end up in the closet, taking up real estate with the other gadgets we were talked into getting. *Oh geez, here we go again, try to focus on something positive. What's my choice, sink or swim?* My decision was always to swim, hoping that one day God would throw me a life jacket.

While waiting for my chiropractor's return, the tiny whisper inside urged me to look up. *Was it intended as an attitude adjustment or to physically look up?* I glanced up. A bulletin board a few feet away had a message on it. *Was it from God's Holy Angels, a reminder that it was Saint Patrick's Day, to hang in there and stick with my kooky sense of humor?* It always got me through hard times. If there was humor in a situation, I would find it, even if I had to dig for it.

The message, written in green, was a line from, *When Irish Eyes Are Smiling*.

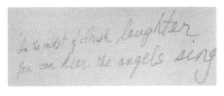

Photo: Bulletin Board message.

When Irish Eyes Are Smiling

There's a tear in your eye, and I'm wondering why,
For it never should be there at all.
With such power in your smile,
Sure, a stone you'd beguile, so there's never a teardrop should fall.
When your sweet lilting laughter's like some fairy song
And your eyes twinkle bright as can be
You should laugh all the while and all other times smile,
And now, smile a smile for me.
When Irish eyes are smiling, sure, 'tis like the morn in Spring
In the lilt of Irish laughter, you can hear the angels sing.
When Irish hearts are happy, all the world seems bright and gay.
And when Irish eyes are smiling, sure, they steal your heart away.
For your smile is a part of the love in your heart,
And it makes even sunshine more bright
Like the linnet's sweet song,
Crooning all the day long
Come your laughter and light.
For the springtime of life is the sweetest of all,
There is ne'er a real care or regret
And while springtime is ours throughout all of youth's hours,
Let us smile each chance we get.

Photo: Christ surrounded by Musician Angels. Hans Memling. 1466. Publc Domain.

The Snow Angels of Manitoba

A TEXT SUDDENLY APPEARED on my cell phone one evening from my best friend Rose, asking for prayers for her son Evan, and his fiancé, Ally. They became stranded inside their car after skidding into a ditch during a blizzard in Souris, Manitoba, while returning home from a weekend trip. Unfortunately, they were not informed about or prepared for the impending storm. It was odd, as Evan traveled on that road before, and knew that he rarely had phone coverage on it. Ally was able to make calls, but Evan could not, although both had the same phones and wireless provider.

The Canadian police did not know when they would be able to get to their location to assist them. Apparently, there were many others who were calling for help. Evan and Ally had already been trapped in the car for two hours. It was very cold, and they were becoming distressed because the car's heater had stopped working.

Luckily, our friend Ric is very skillful with survival tactics. I contacted him, and we texted back and forth his advice to Rose, who relayed the instructions to Evan and Ally. This must have been a terrifying ordeal, as they were thirty miles from the nearest town, in the middle of nowhere without much food or water. The temperature plummeted to seven degrees with blizzard force winds. There was already a foot of snow, and more was rapidly piling up on the ground around them. No other cars

Photo: Snow angel. Story used with permission. 2017.

were on the road. They were totally isolated. Evan kept checking the exhaust pipe to keep it uncovered, which caused his toes to lose feeling from standing in the snow.

For the time being, Rose, Ric, and I continued to text non-stop back and forth until midnight, offering them advice. I prayed that God would send Saint Michael and His Holy Angels to save them. Meanwhile, Ally's mother had a brilliant idea. She went on Facebook and reached out to a group from the nearby area, hoping someone could help them. A few courageous local people answered her plea and put their heads together to construct a plan. I was praying in between texts with my eyes closed and envisioned a car completely covered in snow, down in a ditch when, suddenly, an angel appeared.

The ringtone from Rose's text startled me back to reality. "Good news, someone came, and they are being picked up!"

A man ventured out into the snowstorm with his tractor to rescue them and took them back to his home. His wife prepared a meal for them, and a warm bed. They were welcomed to stay a few more nights until the storm stopped and the roads were safe to travel on. When the highways cleared up, the couple even assisted in towing their car out of the ditch.

The story was on the front page of the town's local newspaper, with photos of Evan and Ally standing behind the brave man who freed them and his lovely wife. The story ended quite happily, as the heroic couple became friends with Evan and Ally, and they stayed in touch.

Rose sent a copy of the newspaper's article to me, and after examining the photos of the heroes I could not help but think something was hidden in them. However, the couple did a fantastic job of concealing their wings, which we knew for certain were safely tucked inside their warm winter coats.

A Man and a Pillow

A Hispanic Center in our area was collecting items for Puerto Rican and Mexican hurricane victims a few years ago. After picking up some items and a few pillows at the store, I took a ride over to make a donation. I entered the office and asked the woman at the desk if they could use some pillows. An elderly gentleman overheard me as he passed by the door. He poked his head into the room, and politely stated how much he desperately needed a new pillow. I hesitated thinking, *These are supposed to be donated to the hurricane victims.*

However, the tiny inner voice said, "Give one to him, there are plenty." Reaching into the bag, I pulled out one of the pillows, handed it over to the man, and said, "You may have one of these, Sir." He thanked me, expressing much gratitude, and looked down lovingly at his new pillow. After a close examination, he became quite elated when he realized it was his favorite brand, size, and material.

As I was leaving, he started a conversation with me in the hallway, telling me he was a volunteer there and had just had pacemaker surgery. It was extremely uncomfortable for him, trying to sleep in his bed without a good pillow, so he was attempting to sleep upright in a chair instead. Residing in a nursing home, he depended on buses to get around, so it was not always convenient for him to get to a store that sold household items. After being invited into his office to chat a few minutes, I learned that, before retirement, he trained young lawyers. Now, years later, he was volunteering to help immigrants.

There were quite a few interesting stories this kind, wise man shared with me. He said it was a miracle I came in that day bringing pillows and called me his special angel. Trying not to laugh, I responded, "No angel, just a vessel God knows how to make use of sometimes" (although I was a bit hesitant at first).

God knew how painful and difficult it was for his dedicated servant to get a good night's rest, so he sent an extra pillow, along with the other donations. God never allows anyone to outdo Him when it comes to giving.

This man was an inspiration and a perfect example. His life consisted of giving to others. I thought about what transpired between the two of us and am confident that he was the angel in this story. Not only did he send me a magnificent message, he also delivered another fine story for these pages. The proof came after sharing some of my life experiences with him and discovering how many of them were linked to the wonderful, angelic events that took place, especially during specific times in my life.

I told him about my devotion to Saint Michael, and how it was accredited to my near-death experience, then said, "It is a miracle I am still around! What could God's plan possibly be for me now?"

A huge grin lit up the tender man's face. He looked me straight in the eye and quoted some famous words from Gracie Allen, "Never put a period where God has put a comma."

Photo: (model) Bob,
Starr Rae's father-in-law.

Angels Watching over Us

O NE SUNNY AFTERNOON, Tommy and I heard something fall onto the windowsill. Thinking it was just one of our electric candles, we figured we would put it back up later, but as the day went on, we forgot about it. The next morning, we discovered my mom had called 911 overnight and was taken by ambulance to the hospital. We rushed over, arriving in time to greet her before she was transferred to a gurney, headed for a colonoscopy. A woman delivering baby roses in a vase, sent by one of my mother's closest friends, made an appearance at the same time. I have said it before and will say it again: "God's Holy Angels have perfect timing."

A dragonfly hovered near us for a few moments that evening, while we were outside watering our plants. We were concerned about my mother's current health status. She had fought cancer like a warrior, on and off since the year 1980, but she was much older now.

Later, on my way to the supermarket, when I stopped at a traffic light, there were three men standing on the corner, holding up a huge white cross. It was unusual, but reassuring. At the entrance to the store was a beautiful display of purplish-blue asters, also called Saint Michael's daisies. Things can pass right over your head if you are not paying close attention. God permits His Holy Angels to send messages to prepare you for various episodes in your life, whether they will be good or bad. After packing the groceries into the back of our car, then exiting the parking lot, I sat at the traffic light waiting for it to turn green. The three men carrying the huge white cross from earlier walked right past the front of the car and each looked directly at me. All of these occurrences seemed to be messages with perfect timing. *Was God trying to get my attention?*

We found out that afternoon that, at the age of eighty-eight, my mom's colon cancer had returned. She endured three resections in the past, but was never treated with radiation or chemotherapy.

This time, the cancer metastasized to her duodenum, a very rare type of cancer. The doctor told us she needed to undergo a huge surgery called a Pancreaticoduodenectomy, or what people would be able to pronounce without tripping over their tongues, The Whipple Procedure. This involved removing cancerous tumors from the head of the pancreas, a portion of the bile duct, the duodenum, the gallbladder, and part of the stomach. The five-year survival rate was 25 percent. Her oncologist was positive about moving forward with the surgery. We prayed Mom would make the right decision.

The next day, Tommy realized it was not an electric candle that fell onto the windowsill in our sunroom the previous day, it was one of our angel suncatchers. It fell the day before my mother called 911. *Was this a warning, or a positive message sent to console us?*

After giving it plenty of thought and weighing her options, my mother consented to the surgery her oncologist recommended, but not to having chemotherapy or radiation, even if it was needed afterward. She recovered from the surgery and rehabilitation and was able to return to independent living in her apartment. But she would have to learn how to live with only a foot of colon. It would not be easy, but she was tough and determined to get her life back to somewhat normal.

Photo: Our Saint Michael statue with some lovely asters.

Saint Michael on the Internet

A TWENTY-SEVEN-YEAR STRETCH OF eight to fifteen chronic migraine headaches per month caused me to desperately seek help. I ping-ponged between countless holistic and western doctors who prescribed umpteen medications that only worked a short while or made the migraines worse.

One of the doctors gave me a prescription for anxiety and depression, which I kept inside a drawer for months. My physical, mental, and spiritual health became seriously on the fritz due to the ongoing misery dominating my head, plus the added stress from my mother's illnesses, plus her previous surgery and rehabilitation.

I asked my sisters and brother in our intercessory prayer group to pray that I would make the right decision about whether or not to fill the prescription. At the time, the small whispering voice inside seemed to be advising me to take it. My worst fear was having a bad withdrawal reaction down the road, while weaning myself off the medication. Long tale short, the prescription was filled, and the whisper's timing could not have been any better than usual.

We watched the months go by and it was time for Mom to visit her oncologist. She was scheduled for another CT scan, as her doctor wanted to make sure the cancer had not returned. Six months had passed since she had the Whipple Procedure. My mind would not stop racing the night before her test, and it turned into another sleepless night of tossing and turning.

The following day, I picked up Mom and took her to the hospital. The test seemed to go well, and she appeared to be in good spirits when we arrived back at her apartment. After a visit, I went home and tried to relax. One of our angel suncatchers fell to the floor, a message and reminder from God's Holy Angels that they would be with us, to be courageous, and to trust in God's will no matter what the future held in store for us. Feeling anxious, we prayed that the anxiety medication would help me. Faith, fortitude, and prudence would be vital to face what might lie ahead if Mom's results came back malignant.

Her oncologist called us in the evening. It was not good news. My mother took the somber news well, believing she could kick the cancer again, but she would have to make a decision on her next course of action. A note appeared on my Facebook page a few hours later. It was from a man named Clement, who is friends with a close longtime friend of mine named Donna. He reached out when he saw my profile photo of Saint Michael.

"Hi! I saw your Archangel profile picture on a mutual friend's thread and thought I'd share a photo of my tattoo with you. My band also did a song with lyrics I wrote titled *Archangel.*"

I could not believe what was on my computer screen. *Did Saint Michael prompt a total stranger, now a friend, to send me an uplifting message to have faith?*

Photo: Clement's tattoo of Saint Michael.
2018. Used with permission.

Feathers, Woodpeckers, and Good Friends

I FOUND TWO WHITE feathers during a morning walk, which was a common incident. Upon arriving back home, I discovered a woodpecker, lying motionless on its side on our patio, which had crashed into our dining room window. Praying it was just dazed from the impact, I spent some time watching over it and protecting it from local predators. When it started to revive, I gave it a dish of water. We became friends for a few minutes, then it flew to a nearby tree and chirped a thank you.

Later in the evening, my mother fell in her bathroom. At this time, she had returned to living in her apartment and had decided to have palliative and hospice care on a daily basis. The hospice nurse who was on call came immediately after my arrival. She wore a beautiful angel necklace, and with a voice as lovely, softly sang *Hail Mary; Gentle Woman*. It calmed both Mom and I while we waited for the ambulance to arrive. Angel statues at the hospice house greeted us as mom was admitted. We both felt the angel's love and reassuring presence.

A few hours after we got Mom settled into a room, I headed back home. Exhaustion was taking over and I needed a good night's rest. Shortly after my arrival, we received a humongous surprise. Mom's closest friends from New Jersey sent a text informing us they were on their way home from vacation, were driving through town, and asked if they could stop by to visit Mom, unaware of the current situation. We were not so sure if it would be a good idea for Mom to receive visitors during such a harrowing time, so we made a call to hospice to inquire about it. Surprisingly, the nurse felt it would be a very positive and uplifting experience for Mom to see her dearest friends at such a distressing time, so they surprised her with a visit.

It was not often that Mom got to see her wonderful and longtime friends, as they lived quite a distance away, so she was delighted when they suddenly made an appearance in her room. The nurse who spoke with me was absolutely right. The visit brought my mother a great deal of joy and comfort. When Tommy and I saw Mom the next day, she was cheerful, and her condition seemed to be leaning toward optimistic. An Angel suncatcher fell from our bedroom window again that night, which did not come as a surprise. We knew it was just a confirmation from God's Holy Angels to rest assured, Mom would be in good hands while staying at hospice.

Yes, they would see to it.

Photo: A rescued woodpecker.

My Mother's Battle with Cancer and Beatific Death

M Y MOTHER WAS a tough woman. She may have been small in stature, but she never tolerated any crap from anyone. More than likely, that was because she had such a difficult and traumatic life since her childhood. The second eldest of seven children, at a young age, she became responsible for assisting her mother with daily chores, plus the raising of her younger brother who had Down syndrome. Needless to say, she did not have much of a childhood.

During the Depression, she lived through, and survived the trauma of, watching her parent's house burn down with the few possessions they owned. Soon after, Mom and her siblings were torn apart from the family and sent away to live with relatives.

After my parents married, Mom had a few miscarriages and gave birth to dead twins while visiting family in Canada. Her babies were immediately taken away to be buried after she gave birth to them, so she never got to see them or feel closure for their loss. Only a wooden cross with a crucifix affixed to it was placed at the grave site to identify it. Sadly, times were much different back then.

Whenever she spoke of it, her voice revealed the suffering that losing her baby boy and girl twins caused her.

As was mentioned in a previous story, my mother moved closer to us many years later when she was in her eighties. We found a beautiful senior apartment not far from where we reside, and she lived independently for almost three years, until the end of her life. When she eventually settled into her new home, she started to volunteer, assisting people who delivered Meals on Wheels to her building, and helped to distribute food packages to tenants who lived there. She also started to attend a Bible study and activities with some of the residents.

Friends agreed that moving was the best decision she ever made. It changed her life, although in the beginning she was terribly unhappy. But, in time, she became friends with the tenants and was loved by many. I finally surrendered to the little whisper that kept coercing me to retire from my job in New Jersey to become my aging mother's full-time caretaker. Luckily, I retired a few months

Photo: Grave site of Starr Rae's brother and sister in New Brunswick, Canada. Sophia D. Used with permission.

prior to her Whipple Procedure, then, six months later, we found out that the cancer again had reared its ugly head.

After the fall in her bathroom and the care she received at the hospice house, Mom was capable of returning to her apartment once again, as she continued with hospice and palliative care. She was getting around fine and resumed her usual activities. Things seemed to be okay, however we were unaware that the cancer had begun to metastasize into her lungs, lymph nodes, and, in a short amount of time, her brain. It was inevitable, and the decline began.

Mom became unable to live alone. Additional help around the clock was needed to provide for her comfort. As Mom's condition worsened, I moved in with her to make sure she received the proper care that she needed. Mom slept in a hospital bed. Her former bed became my bed, which I moved next to hers.

Caretakers came in twenty-four-hours, seven days a week. Many faces came through her door, some good and some not so good. It was an extremely stressful time for us. Nonetheless, leaving my mother alone in her vulnerable condition with total strangers was simply out of the question. God was in control, and we had to trust Him. Fortunately, throughout this course of time, two of the caretakers mom loved earned my trust.

Despite some hardships, we started to observe many miracles and blessings surrounding my mother. Near the end of her life, we witnessed God performing His works through her, and started to perceive challenges as miraculous passages, which allowed Him to enter into our own conflicts and transform them. Through the darkness, pain, and anguish, we knew we would make it past the hard times by keeping focused on our faith.

Everyone involved with Mom noticed how she had a great sense of humor, despite the fact she knew her time on earth was running out.

Her faith, strength, and courage inspired all in her presence. One evening, Colleen, one of Mom's exceptional caretakers, sent me home to shower and get a change of clothes. It was difficult to leave Mom alone with people we did not know, however Colleen was one of Mom's favorite caretakers. She had earned my confidence and convinced me it would be safe to go home for a shower and to have dinner with my husband in our own home.

Photo: Painting of Saint Michael from The Basilica of Saint Michael. Miramichi, New Brunswick, Canada. Used with permission

It felt good to get away for a short while. After being refreshed and enjoying a home-cooked meal, I returned to Mom's bedside. Her condition had become a downward spiral. She would need me by her side now, more than ever.

Upon my return, Colleen was in the living room. She said that after I left, Mom called out,

"Colleen, I'm ready to go!" Colleen shouted back, "You are ready to go where?"

Mom replied, "To the funeral home!" Colleen, trying not to laugh said,

"But you're not dead yet!" Mom responded,

"Well then, can you put on Dr. Phil for me?!"

We had some good laughs, which eased the tension for a while, but Mom's cancer progressed and she deteriorated. Near the end, she blew kisses and became very loving to anyone who visited. She shared her visions with us, of seeing beautiful flowers and Jesus lying across the road in front of her. He told her he was not ready for her yet, so she told us she jumped over him! She also told us that she saw little people at the foot of her bed.

What was my mother seeing? Cherubs? Maybe her twins?

We sensed that her time was coming, and did everything to make her feel as comfortable as possible. The television was on twenty-four hours a day in her room, mostly on EWTN, a Catholic channel. We felt it would be consoling for her to hear prayers, specifically when we were not nearby. Colleen mentioned that Mom could hear prayers subconsciously while she slept.

The night Mom passed away, Charlene, another one of Mom's favorite caretakers, was scheduled to stay overnight with us. She gave Mom a special treat, a massage with her favorite lavender body lotion after she gave her a bath, so Mom was clean and refreshed for the evening.

Mass came on EWTN, and the three of us stayed up to watch it. Although totally exhausted from lack of sleep at this point, I was determined to stay awake until the Mass was over, then, I fell asleep.

It was close to midnight when Charlene came over to alert me that Mom was getting ready for the journey to her heavenly home. We both sat next to Mom, one on each side, holding her hands and assuring her it was okay to go. Mom told me she loved me and apologized for not always being a good mother. I told her I loved her also, then apologized for not always being a good daughter. I told her to have faith that we would be together again one day and God would make sure everything would be perfect the next time. There would be no more pain or lack of understanding, the things that caused us to suffer physically, mentally, spiritually, and emotionally while we lived our lives here on earth.

I realized how blessed we had been. We had made it through an extremely difficult time together and were able to make amends before saying goodbye.

Mom passed away on September 12, 2015, around 1:00 a.m., as I held her hand and recited our beloved Saint Michael prayer. At the conclusion of the prayer, she set her eyes upon me and peacefully let out her last breath.

The image of Saint Michael appeared on the TV again, and I caught a glimpse of it before letting go of my mother's hand, knowing he had responded to our prayers and came swiftly to guide and protect her soul from the attacks of the enemy. I accepted his image as a message of comfort.

The coroner arrived not long afterward to pronounce Mom's death. The little voice inside told me to look at the television. Once again, EWTN had the image of Saint Michael on the screen. It was only for a moment, but long enough for all of us to see it. I was convinced that Mom, who also had a deep devotion to Saint Michael, was accompanied by his Divine Assistance to the Gates of Paradise. While Charlene and I stood there with the coroner, the clock struck. It was 3:00 a.m..

Forever rest in peace mom.

Photo: Starr Rae's mother on her eighty-eighth birthday. 2015.

Bagpipes and Grasshoppers

N OT LONG AFTER Mom's death, Tommy and I went to a Celtic Festival. When we heard the bagpipes, we turned back, as the sound of it got to me. A year earlier, we had taken Mom there to see the bagpipers, Irish dancers, and the cultural events. She was so proud of our Scottish ancestry, and wore my dad's Cameron Highlander's beret from when he was in the Army. The festival brought many mixed emotions that I was not ready to face, so back to the car we headed.

Walking down the hill to the parking lot, we saw a grasshopper sitting on top of a fence and noticed it was missing a leg. It came right up to us, allowing us to take photos of it. This was out of the ordinary, as it did not hop away and seemed to trust us and enjoy being our model for a photo shoot. After taking a couple of shots, it hopped aboard some tree bark I offered it, and allowed me to transport it to the grass, then off it went into the bushes.

The encounter really lifted my spirits. *Did Mom send a message through this grasshopper?* Despite its disability, it moved around fine and seemed content. Was there a connection?

I envisioned Mom reveling to the skirl of her beloved pipes being played in Heaven. Next to her was a fine young lad, wearing a kilt matching the plaid on the beret she felt so honored to wear.

Photos: (Top) Starr Rae's Mom. (below) A friendly grasshopper.

Message from a Cardinal

DURING THE JANUARY blizzard of 2016, our town was being bombarded by thirty-one inches of snow. As we lay in bed that morning, I prayed that Mom was happy and at peace in Heaven. We prayed every day for the repose of her soul, hoping she was at eternal rest in the presence of God. Mom had passed away the previous September.

If only there was a way for her to let us know she was at peace.

A flock of male cardinals, very bright in color, especially against the white snow, were in our backyard, socializing around the birdbath and bird feeders. Mom loved cardinals and often received cardinal-themed gifts. I motioned to Tommy to look at the cardinals, then asked, "Is this a message from Mom?"

Laughing, he said, "We get cardinals in our yard all the time."

I responded, "You're right."

Later that day, an email came from our friend Linda, who has a keen interest in photography. She goes on day trips with her boyfriend, Wes, to take beautiful photos of different types of birds in their natural habitat. The previous day, she had taken photos of birds in her backyard and was motivated to send us one of her cardinal photos.

Photo: Cardinal. Linda S. Used with permission.

It had to be from Mom! Its stern facial expression was similar to one she often wore while quoting a favorite phrase she used a lot, especially while I was growing up,

"For the love of God! You're like a bull in a china closet!"

The Copper Bracelet

T OMMY AND I love to walk around downtown areas, where there is usually an abundance of delightful stores to explore and a variety of cafes that are pleasing to the palate. We were browsing one day in a gift shop and were drawn to some copper bracelets. Mom owned one and swore it helped her arthritis go away. A very pretty bracelet stood out, so we bought it.

An elderly woman working at the cash register appeared close to Mom's age. Mom was eighty-eight when she passed away. The clerk wore a gold cross with a thin, sparkly gold chain identical to the cross and chain that Mom wore. Since Mom passed away, I have been wearing it and have never taken it off. The woman noticed the cross and chain right away, and we marveled over it after a close-up comparison. She could not recall where she got hers, but knew that it was very old. Neither one of us had seen another one like it until that day.

It was Tommy's birthday, so the two of us celebrated over a delicious dinner at a restaurant recommended by a friend. At the entrance was a decorative red cardinal, and a cross was mounted on the wall behind our table with a gold Cherubim.

The next day, Linda sent another cardinal photo, but this time it was one her boyfriend, Wes, had taken. It was sent with a note attached:

"Your mother is everywhere!"

Photo: (Left) Copper bracelet. (Right) Cardinal. Wes H. Used with permission.

Message in the Sky

I NEEDED TO SCHEDULE another biopsy, which sent a reality check and reminder of how Mom stood so bravely all those years, taking up her gauntlet, that lasted so long. It saddened everyone that she eventually lost her fight and succumbed to colon cancer after holding out for as long as she could, fighting the good fight right up to the end. She was a true warrior. Her suffering lasted a very long time, but she never lost faith in God. If only I possessed a quarter of her courage and strength.

The Lord knows about our weaknesses, and how easy it is for us to forget that He is still up there in charge of everything. All he asks of us is to trust in Him. Because He is omniscient, omnipotent, and omnipresent, He knows everything about us. Regardless of our sinfulness, He still loves us unconditionally and is merciful, even when we do not deserve it. I believe this is why He allows His Holy Angels to send these elevating and miraculous messages to us at times. He knows we forget and can use reminders, especially when the evil spirits are doing their best to send anguish into our lives and we start to lose faith and become despondent.

Photo: Message in the sky. Diane R. Used with permission.

On countless occasions in the past, I have tried to figure out His reason for allowing these mystical and beneficial events to transpire, and this was the only answer I could think of that made perfect sense. It must not be an easy or pleasant assignment that He has given to His Holy Angels! Some of the humans He created can be very complex, not always easy to contend with, stubborn, arrogant, and wayfaring. He knows we all could use some help. Angels must be pretty darn patient, smart, and creative from having to deal with some of us, especially with the ones who can be a tad bit off the wall—I suppose you could say someone like me!

Diane, who is a close friend of mine from my intercessory prayer group, sent me a text one morning while she was in Florida. Unaware of the biopsy I was scheduled to have in the afternoon, she was sitting outside enjoying the warmth, fresh air, and her surroundings. She happened to look up at the sky, noticed something extraordinary, and took a photo of it.

Afterward, she received a strong feeling (a whisper?!) to share it with me. The sun was shining brightly against a pretty blue sky, and five white letters came into view, a message undisputable, spelling "Trust!" There it was, the key word, written in the heavens!

It reminded me of when Jesus and his disciples were in a boat on the lake and a violent storm came upon them. Jesus was sound asleep, and they woke him in fear. He said to them,

"Why are you terrified, O you of little faith?" Then he got up, rebuked the winds and the sea, and there was great calm. (Matthew 8:26) (NABRE).

"I love you, Lord, my strength, Lord my rock. my fortress, my deliverer. My God, my rock of refuge, my shield, my saving horn, my stronghold! Praised be the Lord, I exclaim! I have been delivered from my enemies. The cords of death encompassed me; the torrents of destruction terrified me. The cords of Sheol encircled me; the snares of death lay in wait for me. In my distress I called out: Lord! I cried out to my God. From his temple he heard my voice; my cry to him reached his ears." (Psalm 18:2–7) (NABRE).

Angel in the Waiting Room

F RUSTRATED OVER AN unresolved issue caused by a doctor's care-less staff, a ten-minute drive to the doctor's office turned into a forty-five-minute traffic jam before my arrival. The staff told me the issue would still not be resolved until the following day. I sat in the waiting room, steaming and trying to calm myself down. This was my third attempt to straighten out their stupid mistake. A woman entered the waiting room and sat next to me. This was odd, as there was only one other person waiting beside myself, and there were plenty of chairs. She could have sat anywhere. Why did she sit next to me?

She started to pray "The Our Father," just loud enough for me to hear. I looked up at her and smiled, sensing the angels had sent her to calm my shattered nerves, then bowed my head and silently joined in the prayer with her. My anger abated, then a voice called out my name, summoning me into the office to settle the dispute. I rose, turned toward the woman, smiled, and said, "Thank you."

She was still sitting in the waiting room when the staff finished resolving the issue with me and motioned me to come over to her. She put a few small pieces of cloth in my hand and said they were touched by several relics at a Shrine. She assured me everything would be okay, to keep praying, hold onto my faith, and God would take good care of me. We began to talk and shared some of our life experiences with each other. I told her about my book of angel experiences which was underway and, hopefully, would be published one day. She was delighted to hear the encounter we were currently engaging in would be included in my stories.

We had much in common and made an instant connection. Both of our mothers were devoted to Padre Pio. My mother was born in February, and her mother passed away in February. After sharing some miraculous stories, she showed me a photo of an X-ray of her leg, which had been broken in several places from a car accident. The doctors told her she would never be able to walk again, but she refused to believe them and was miraculously healed, fully able to walk, as if the accident had never happened.

She also had Lyme disease, which affected her optic nerve, and was told by a few eye doctors she would become blind. Again, she refused to believe them, and her vision is perfectly fine. Before leaving the office, we gave each other a big hug. A warm sensation swept over me, and I instantly knew she was a blessing sent from God in disguise. God knows when comfort is required and exactly when to send one of His Earth Angels. This was definitely another one of those occasions.

Realizing it was getting close to rush hour, I started to feel concerned, saying that it would be best for me to head back home to avoid the traffic.

"Do not worry, there will not be any traffic," she said with certainty in her smile. She was right! There was not much traffic, and the drive back home was actually pleasant. A peaceful feeling enveloped me, as I became aware that God's Grace came to visit me in a place where it was most needed, inside a doctor's waiting room.

Photo: The Angel of Nisky Cemetery,
Bethlehem, Pennsylvania.
Used with permission.

Lest You Dash Yourself

I WOUND UP DOING a face plant on a bike trail a few years ago. Luckily, there were no witnesses besides my husband and no broken bones, just a few bruised ribs, a sprained hand, a bloody knee, and, again, wounded pride. It is a good idea to wear a helmet while riding a bike, especially if you are me. A friend once advised Tommy to buy me a suit of armor, because I tend to be so accident-prone.

Yet, in spite of being so spasmodic, I am resilient, and give it my best shot to make a comeback with as little drama as possible. My plan consists of dusting myself off, trying to laugh in the face of adversity, then feigning that nothing is wrong (a gut effort now and then). Time has proven this effective, mostly to spare myself embarrassment. There is nothing worse than a handful or more of spectators witnessing your calamity after taking a nosedive, then lying sprawled on the gravel bawling like a baby.

Photo: Starr Rae about to perform a precarious move.

One particular day of catastrophe, my plan got kicked into high gear, as I psyched myself into riding my bike back to the car, despite the carnage I had just done to myself.

The four miles seemed to take forever. Only by the Grace of God did I have the ability to make it back, between smothered bouts of shrieking, which I kept hidden from my poor worried husband.

God's Holy Angels must be watching over me twenty-four hours a day, seven days a week, shaking their heads in disbelief.

We felt their presence that day, no doubt.

I was riding at a pace of thirteen miles per hour when the crash occurred, so my injuries could have been a lot worse.

The Mysterious Angel Card

T OMMY AND I attended a wake to offer condolences to our friend Heather, who had lost her aunt. There was a long line of visitors signing in at the prayer-card stand. We noticed a card on it that was separate and unlike the others, as it was very colorful and stood out.

It was interesting that no one else decided to take it. Taking a closer look, the image on it appeared to be Saint Michael. *Where in the world did it come from and why was it there alone by itself?* We had been to many Catholic wakes and never saw a card like this one. All of the cards we saw in the past either had pictures of Jesus, Mary, or a photo of the deceased.

Photo: The mysterious angel card. Origin unknown.

Afterward, we went to the pharmacy and were told my prescription would take three days. Not realizing the prescription had ran out, I needed it that night.

Back home, a message was on our answering machine. Luckily, the pharmacy found some of the medication, and it was waiting to be picked up.

Tommy reminded me about the angel card.

I called the funeral home to inquire about it, and the woman who answered the phone was clueless about where it came from, and said she would investigate it, then call us back, but she never did.

A friend told us the words on the card were Russian for Archangel Michael.

Various Occurrences

H ERE ARE A few other incidents that occurred in the past couple of years where there have been other witnesses who, without a doubt, also believe these events confirm the presence of God's Holy Messengers' activity in our lives.

Do angels like to be seen on TV? Often, when the television is turned on to EWTN, the image of Saint Michael appears on the screen or the prayer to Saint Michael is about to begin.

Does God send His Holy angels to deliver us mainly when we are sinking into despair, or when we need to seriously chill out? God's Earth Angels have been known to drop in when we are frustrated or angry. A good example would be someone who suddenly appears to help us through an incomprehensible website. *God, please help me figure out how to write and publish this book!*

Can angels drive a car on their wings? A few days before our car went in for inspection, an angel light came on the dashboard. After checking the front passenger tire, it had a slow leak. When the car arrived at the mechanic's, there were three nails in that tire, yet we got there without a problem.

Can you receive blessings from the angels? One of my favorite clients gave me a cute little solar-powered angel on the day I retired from my job in New Jersey. When the sun shines she flaps her wings, a reminder of the many blessings received while serving all of my wonderful clients throughout the years. Some of these clients even became Earth Angels.

Can angels communicate through electricity? Once during an intercessory prayer group meeting, we had just finished saying the Saint Michael prayer when the air conditioner turned itself on. How strange, especially because it was in the middle of January! We also experienced lights flickering while doing *Lectio Divina* or after we ended a group discussion. Once, after we recited the *Come Holy Spirit* prayer, Siri's voice responded from my cell phone, "Hello!"

Do angels like to travel? We took a trip one weekend and came across beautiful angel banners and a beautiful painting of a fox. Earlier in the week, a pretty red fox was in our backyard sunning itself in our rock garden. It kept returning to the same spot for a few days and did not seem to mind having its photo taken.

Many different animals enjoy spending time in our yard, including groundhogs, deer, birds, chipmunks, and the neighborhoods feral cats. None appear to be afraid of us. Some have even peeked inside our sunroom windows, listened to music on the radio, or come closer to the house when we jam. Occasionally at night, we hear an owl hooting from one of our trees. Once, we saw it during the day, and it was close enough to photograph.

Photo: A pretty red fox.

A Visit to Saint Michael's Basilica

W HAT GOOD FORTUNE it was when we were able to visit Saint Michael's Basilica, located in Miramichi, New Brunswick, Canada, during the course of our journey to visit family.

Behind schedule, we arrived on a Monday afternoon and were grievously aware that the Basilica was not open on Mondays. Although we were sad about not being able to go inside to view the beautiful shrine, we were still very grateful to be there. At least we could wander the grounds, say a prayer on the front steps, and take photos of the gorgeous exterior architecture before heading to our next destination. We parked our car and walked toward the front of the Basilica.

From out of nowhere, a man suddenly appeared, opened the side door to the Basilica, and entered. Without a moment to spare, I grabbed Tommy's arm and dragged him along with me to the inside of the Basilica. *Wahoo! Game on!*

Once inside, we found ourselves standing in front of the altar, looking up at an enormous three-paneled altarpiece with a beautiful painting of Saint Michael in the center.

Photo: Altarpiece inside The Basilica of Saint Michael. Miramichi, New Brunswick, Canada. Starr Rae Knighte. Used with permission.

Consumed by emotion, tears started running down my face. It took several minutes before the profound experience started to diminish. We were the only ones inside the Basilica. The man who entered before us was nowhere in sight and had mysteriously vanished.

Sitting in the front pew, we offered prayers and thanksgiving to God for allowing us entrance into Saint Michael's beautiful sanctuary. He knew how much this meant, and that it was a phenomenal experience neither one of us would ever forget. We walked around, taking plenty of photos inside the Basilica, then proceeded to go outside and take just as many. If we had taken a million photos, it still would not have been enough.

I am not paying for all of that iCloud storage for nothing!

Two grateful hearts continued the journey to our next destination. The family visit was destined to be heartwarming and filled with many blessings. Fifteen years had passed since we last saw my aunts and uncle, and it had been many more years for some cousins who had since become grandparents. I had not seen several of my cousins

Photo: The Basilica of Saint Michael, Miramichi, New Brunswick, Canada. Used with permission.

since childhood. My own ongoing health issues, plus Mom's cancer, made travel inconceivable at that time.

Everyone reconnected instantly. The time spent with them was momentous and truly treasured. It was wonderful to see everyone after all those long years, and it felt like a warm welcome back home for both of us, after a tremendously long journey.

Tommy was welcomed with open arms by my family members who had not met him yet, and he instantly felt like part of our family.

Distance may come between us for a while, but our hearts remain linked together.

In Loving Memory of Pam

I T WAS A cold winter morning, and it snowed until early afternoon. Feelings of sadness and depression kept company with me like an unwanted intruder. Many of us were mourning the loss of our dear friend, Pam, who had suddenly and unexpectedly passed away from a pulmonary embolism a few months earlier. We were all still in a state of shock. It was like a terrible dream that would never come to an end, one we could not wake up from and feel relieved that it was not real. It was difficult to believe that Pam was no longer with us, yet the final, harsh reality had started to set in. To make matters worse, April, another one of our closest friends, was moving to South Dakota in the next two days.

Photo: Sun breaking through the clouds.

Halfheartedly, I suited up for the cold, then headed out for a walk, struggling to fight the sadness inside my heart. Spending time outdoors, walking and talking to God, tended to push me onward. The connection with nature never failed to bring some kind of comfort.

After inserting my earbuds and setting my fitness tracker, the tiny whisper inside prompted me to listen to some favorite tunes. *Maybe they would lift my spirit.* Through experience, I have found music to be very healing, and lyrics can speak volumes.

One particular song made me think of Heaven. I looked up at the overcast sky and questioned God. *Where do we go from here?* It was meant in general, but it also referred to my own life.

The song was suddenly interrupted by a text from our friend Dan. He sent a photo that I had requested a while ago of Pam, his beloved wife. I texted back,

"Beautiful angel."

The sun immediately broke through the clouds, shining with warmth upon my face. *Did Pam send a message not to be sad, to let us know that Heaven is real, and to look upward, beyond the clouds?* It was remarkable that Dan sent her photo at that specific time, the moment the sun came out!

There is no uncertainty in my mind that our dear friend Pam is up there cooking one of her famous and fabulous feasts for God and His Holy Angels, while hosting one of her incredibly awesome themed parties. She was second to none when it came to entertaining, being hospitable, and giving to those she loved, especially Dan, the one she adored. We could envision her afterward, singing karaoke in perfect, blissful harmony with the choir of angels and saints while joyfully dancing amongst the stars.

Photo: Pam. Photo by Dan B.
Used with permission.

Feathers and Block Party Angels Revisited

F OUR YEARS HAD passed since the fateful Fourth of July block party when my neighbor convinced me to publish these stories. A white feather was perfectly centered on my pillow as we rose from bed that morning.

Our pillows and bedding are encased, plus our pillows have pillowcases, so how did a feather wind up on my pillow and not cling to my hair? It was clearly meant to be seen, a message to trust God's will, that the effort to get these stories edited, published, and directed into the public would, sooner or later, come to completion.

It was predestined to take a few more years of coping with conflicts sent from the enemy, who must have basked in delight at my setbacks and feelings of defeat, which for a while were many.

From my perspective, he advanced way ahead of me with many hindering strategies. It felt like being involved in a tug of war between good and evil, but I was shown how to accomplish this mission because I never gave up.

I trusted God and learned that we were not created by God to be His drivers, we were created to be His passengers.

"I can do all things through Christ who strengthens me."
(Philippians 4:13) (NKJV)

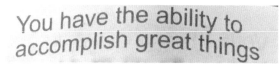

Photo: Fortune cookie message.

In Loving Memory of
Janet and Richie

P EOPLE COME INTO your life for a reason, a season, or a lifetime. Two very special people were in my life for more than twenty-five years. Anyone in the company of Janet and Richie were blessed to be in the midst of two of God's Holiest Earth Angels.

Janet suffered from multiple sclerosis and was confined to bed for approximately thirty-five years. When I met her, she only had mobility of her left arm, and relied on others to do everything for her.

Her husband, Richie, retired from his job early to become her full-time caretaker. He did all of the housework, cooking, shopping, bill paying, nursing, and so on. He was so loving and devoted to his wife and had such tremendous faith in God, despite the constant trials that were sent to him and Janet. Richie had quite a few physical problems himself. Diabetes, an aneurysm in his brain, and he was also in the early stages of multiple sclerosis. He aged terribly fast, and looked a lot older than he was. When he was in his early sixties, he looked like he was in his late eighties.

Janet and Richie lived in a small, ranch-style home with humble surroundings and owned a small twenty-one-inch television set, which was their only companionship. They watched it together most of their days, in a little room where they slept in separate beds. Janet could barely see the television, even with her glasses on, due to her disease, which caused double vision. Richie slept on a cot in the corner of the room to always be near her, in case she needed him, and rarely left her side unless he went to church, had to go food shopping, or go to the doctor.

When I first started to visit them, Richie used a hoist to pick Janet up from her bed and swing her over into her wheelchair so she could go to church with him. It was a real treat for Janet, as she did not go out often. Richie was able to take her on more outings after he bought a van for the disabled. He drove while she sat in her wheelchair, firmly locked into the passenger side. Unfortunately, this ended when Richie accidentally dropped Janet one day and broke her leg.

Their house had narrow hallways, so Richie gave up washing Janet in the bathtub. Her wheelchair could barely fit inside their tiny bathroom, so he resorted to giving her sponge baths in bed instead. Eventually, as the years passed, they both became homebound. There was no family around to help them. Janet was an only child, who lost both of her parents years ago, and the family Richie had left rarely visited them. I met these two through the church bulletin at my former parish and through my best friend, Rose, who was already visiting them at the time.

Janet needed volunteers to visit, and stretch her arms and legs to relieve the pain and stiffness she suffered as a result of the MS. After a few years, due to a bad back, I had to stop doing therapy for Janet, but continued to visit. Rose and I developed a unique relationship with them, and our bond strengthened over the years. The four of us became very close friends. We were always there for each other during the good times, and we stuck it out through the worst.

When Tommy and I moved to Pennsylvania, Janet and Richie were afraid they would never see me again, but I assured them,

"Do not worry, I'm like poison ivy, very hard to get rid of!"

Janet needed her fix every now and then: a Hershey's chocolate bar. It was the only thing this incredible woman ever asked for. She was always so cheerful, even when things were the infinite pits. Once, I went to buy her a chocolate bar and was embarrassed to find there was no money in my wallet. The angels cued me to look in the car, where I found a dollar bill neatly folded up where we keep our loose change. It was clearly meant for Janet.

Her face immediately lit up if she saw her favorite dark chocolate candy bar, one of the few things left in life she could really enjoy.

Janet and Richie were a couple filled with incredible courage, strength, dignity, and an absolute lack of self-pity. These two heavenly stars brightened our days, warmed our hearts, and deeply inspired our lives. They always put smiles on our faces. There was never a shortage of laughter in their house, but, like most married couples, Richie could really get Janet ticked off, and holy smokes, would she give him a piece of her mind. Then, after a few minutes, she would laugh that good-hearted laugh along with us, and the moment was over.

Once, I talked Richie into letting me cut his hair into a Mohawk. Because he was so conserva-tive, I nearly went into shock when he allowed me to go ahead and do it, then slop on some gel and take a photo of his new coiffure. I stood back, took a good look at my creation, and thought to myself, *Dear God, it looks like Richie has a dorsal fin. Janet is going to have a cow!*

Photo: Richie with a mohawk and Richie's usual hairstyle

I was lucky to sidestep a tongue lashing. All she said was, "Clean him up! Make him spiffy again!"

Richie was like a father to me. We could talk about anything. He was quite a character, who joked around often and had a terrific sense of humor. It was easy to be myself around Richie and Janet. There were no worries about being judged as being too this or too that, or being put down for having silly behaviors at times. They whole-heartedly and unconditionally loved and accepted me, 100 percent, for who I was from day one. I felt warmly welcomed and at home with them.

Occasionally, Richie and I would go off on each other, mostly when he was being stubborn. Janet had no problem calling him out,

"You pigheaded ~bleep~!"

Then there was silence. A few minutes would pass, things would cool down, and one of us would burst out in laugher (usually me!). Everything was in good fun, and done with only trust and love.

Richie always tried to give me and Rose money for things we did for them and got worked up if we did not accept it. Once he even threatened that if we did not accept his money, he would never let us back into their house!

Rose and I looked at each other and tried not to laugh out loud. He must have forgotten he had given both of us keys!

With much sadness, we lost Janet after her courageous battle with MS at the age of sixty-nine, on April 22, 2019. Soon after, Rose and I tried to prepare for the inevitability of Richie's increasingly poor health.

The heartbreaking reality came a few months later on September 30, 2019, the day after Michaelmas, when he suddenly passed away at the age of eighty, more likely from a broken heart than anything else.

It was very hard for Rose and I, so soon after losing Janet, because this extraordinary couple made such an impact on us and became such an important and special part of our lives.

They are terribly missed.

Despite all of the hardships and boundless suffering endured, neither one of them ever lost their faith. Their moral compass was permanently set, and their undying love for each other was nothing less than perfect.

Rose and I are certain the gates to Heaven were flung wide open by God's Holy Angels as these two unsung saints departed from the earth. Then, upon their arrival, God, along with His Holy Angels, saints, and Saint Michael, escorted them into the heavenly banquet.

Afterward, they were led out onto the greatest polka dance floor ever created.

Photo: Left to right: Richie,
Rose, Janet, and Starr Rae.

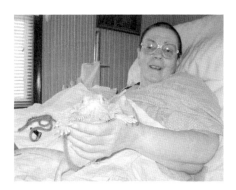

Photo: Janet with Draco Dracaena.
Janet loved our bearded dragons so much!
They brightened her day and loved cuddling with her,
which always made her smile. 2007.

The Saint Michael Prayer

Saint Michael the Archangel, defend us in battle.
Be our protection against the wickedness and snares of the devil
May God rebuke him, we humbly pray;
and do thou, O Prince of the Heavenly Host,
by the Power of God, cast into hell Satan
and all the evil spirits who roam throughout the world
seeking the ruin of souls. Amen.

A bit of history on the Saint Michael Prayer:

This prayer was composed by Pope Leo XIII in the 1800s after he had a frightening vision of demonic spirits threatening to destroy the Church. This occurred while he celebrated mass, causing him to become pale and very shaken. It prompted him to write the prayer afterward to combat the presence of evil in our lives.

Photo: Saint Michael the Archangel statue. Located at The Basilica of the National Shrine of Mary, Queen of the Universe. Orlando, Florida. Diane R. Used with permission.

The Chaplet of Saint Michael (Rosary of the Angels)

O God, come to my aid, O Lord make haste to help me.

Glory be to the Father, and to the son, and to the Holy Spirit, as it was in the beginning, is now and ever shall be world without end, Amen.

Say one Our Father and three Hail Marys after each of the nine salutations in honor of the nine Choir of Angels, as follows.

First Salutation: Through the intercession of Saint Michael and the celestial Choir of Seraphim, may the Lord make us worthy to burn with the fire of perfect charity. Amen.

Second Salutation: Through the intercession of Saint Michael and the celestial Choir of Cherubim, may God grant us the grace to abandon the ways of sin and follow the path of Christian perfection. Amen.

Third Salutation: Through the intercession of Saint Michael and the celestial Choir of Thrones, may the Lord infuse into our hearts a true and earnest spirit of humility. Amen.

Fourth Salutation: Through the intercession of Saint Michael and the celestial Choir of Dominations, may it please God to grant us the grace to have dominion over our senses and to correct our depraved passions. Amen.

Fifth Salutation: Through the intercession of Saint Michael and the celestial Choir of Virtues, may our Lord keep us from falling into temptation and deliver us from evil. Amen.

Sixth Salutation: Through the intercession of Saint Michael and the celestial Choir of Powers, may God vouchsafe to keep our soul from the wiles and the temptations of the devil. Amen.

Seventh Salutation: Through the intercession of Saint Michael and the celestial Choir of Principalities, may it please God to fill our hearts with the spirit of true and hearty obedience. Amen.

Eighth Salutation: Through the intercession of Saint Michael and the celestial Choir of Archangels, may it please God to grant us the grace of perseverance in the faith and in all good works, that we may thereby be enabled to attain the glory of paradise. Amen.

Ninth Salutation: Through the intercession of Saint Michael and the celestial Choir of Angels, may God vouchsafe to grant that they may protect us during life, and after death, may lead us to the everlasting glory of heaven. Amen.

At the conclusion, say an Our Father in honor of Saint Michael, an Our Father in honor of Saint Gabriel, an Our Father in honor of Saint Raphael, and an Our Father to honor our Guardian Angel.

End the Chaplet with the following prayer: Michael glorious prince, chief and champion of the heavenly hosts, guardian of the souls of men, conqueror of the rebellious angels, steward of the palace of God under our divine king, Jesus Christ, our worthy leader, endowed with superhuman excellence and virtues, vouchsafe to free us from all evil, who with full confidence have recourse to thee; and by thy incomparable protection enable us to make progress every day in the faithful service of our God. Amen.

Pray for us, most blessed Michael, Prince of the Church of Jesus Christ. That we may be made worthy of his promises.

Almighty and Eternal God, who in thine own marvelous goodness and pity didst, for the common salvation of man, choose Thy glorious Archangel Michael to be the prince of Thy church, make us worthy we pray Thee, to be delivered by his beneficent protection from all our enemies, that, at the hour of our death, none of them may approach to harm us, rather do Thou vouchsafe onto us that by the same Archangel Michael, we may be introduced into the presence of Thy most high and divine majesty. Through the merits of the same Jesus Christ our Lord. Amen.

A bit of history on the Chaplet:

In the 1700s, a nun named Antonia d'Astonac had a vision of Saint Michael requesting to be honored by reciting salutations to each of the nine Choirs of Angels. In turn, he would escort those doing the devotion to Holy Communion with nine angels from each choir. Reciting it every day guaranteed his constant aid with the holy angels and deliverance from purgatory, including their loved ones.

Photo: Cherubs from BL Royal 6 E IX, f. 6- PICRYL Public domain.

Angel of God Prayer

Angel of God, my guardian dear,
to whom God's love commits me here;
Ever this day be at my side,
to light and guard, to rule and guide. Amen.

Photo: The Guardian Angel. Antonio Franchi, known as il Lucchese. 1653.
Museo Civico, Riva del Garda. Public Domain.

Photo: Feather.

"For our struggle is not with flesh and blood
but with the principalities, with the powers,
with the world rulers of this present darkness,
with the evil spirits in the heavens.
Therefore, put on the armor of God,
that you may be able to resist on the evil day
and, having done everything, to hold your ground.
So stand fast with your loins girded in truth,
clothed with righteousness as a breastplate,
and your feet shod in readiness for the gospel of peace.
In all circumstances, hold faith as a shield,
to quench all the flaming arrows of the evil one.
And take the helmet of salvation and the sword of the spirit,
which is the word of God." (Ephesians 6:12-17) (NABRE).

About the Author

AFTER TWENTY-FIVE YEARS of journaling true stories of her personal angelic experiences in a diary and surviving a near-death encounter, Starr Rae received a calling to fulfill a mission in writing a book to share her eye-opening stories of faith and hope.

God, His Holy Angels, and some Earth Angels became paramount in the guidance required for her first book to be completed and published.

Born and raised a Jersey Girl, her heart is divided between her home state and current beloved town, which is nestled in the state of Pennsylvania.

Her hobbies include photography, hiking, biking (when not face planting), rock hounding, costuming/theatrical makeup, singing, karaoke, and learning bass guitar so she can jam with her husband, Tommy, a rock guitarist of many years.

Photo: Starr Rae and Tommy. Taken at Sioux Falls, South Dakota. April R. Used with permission.

"Do not forget to entertain strangers
for by doing so some have unwittingly entertained angels."
(Hebrews 13:2) (NKJV).

Photo: Tobias Farewell to the Angel. Giovanni Bilivert. 17th Century. Public Domain.

*Front and back cover photos by Starr Rae Knighte. The statue of Saint Michael the Archangel located on The Campus of The National Centre for Padre Pio, Barto, Pennsylvania. Used with permission.